THE
JAMES SPRUNT STUDIES
IN HISTORY
AND POLITICAL SCIENCE

*Published under the Direction of
the Departments of History and Political Science
of The University of North Carolina at Chapel Hill*

VOLUME 54

Editors

J. CARLYLE SITTERSON, *Chairman*
FEDERICO G. GIL
JOHN D. MARTZ
GEORGE V. TAYLOR
GEORGE B. TINDALL

THE RECONSTRUCTION OF EDWARD A. POLLARD

A REBEL'S CONVERSION
TO POSTBELLUM UNIONISM

by
Jack P. Maddex, Jr.

CHAPEL HILL
THE UNIVERSITY OF NORTH CAROLINA PRESS
1974

Copyright © 1974 by
The University of North Carolina Press
All rights reserved
Manufactured in the United States of America
ISBN 0-8078-5054-3
Library of Congress Catalog Card Number 74-8961

Library of Congress Cataloging in Publication Data

Maddex, Jack P 1941-
  The reconstruction of Edward A. Pollard.

  (The James Sprunt studies in history and political science, v. 54)
  Bibliography: p.
  1. Pollard, Edward Alfred, 1831-1872. I. Title.
II. Series.
F214.P572M32   975.5'04'0924   74-8961
ISBN 0-8078-5054-3

Dedicated
to George Tindall

". . . [N]othing is hid that shall not be made manifest, nor anything secret that shall not be known and come to light."
—Luke 8: 17

TABLE OF CONTENTS

	Acknowledgments	ix
I	The Two Worlds of Edward A. Pollard	3
II	The Old South Creed, 1832-1867	24
III	A Disguised Surrender, 1867-1868	43
IV	The Reconstructed Rebel, 1868-1872	62
V	Conclusions and Implications	80
	Notes	85
	Bibliography	97
	Index	107

ACKNOWLEDGMENTS

Many friends have kindly read and criticized drafts of parts of this monograph. Among my colleagues at the University of Oregon, I wish to thank Professors Thomas P. Govan, Raymond Birn, and Thomas A. Brady. Others to whom I am indebted for criticisms are Professors George B. Tindall and Joel R. Williamson of the University of North Carolina at Chapel Hill; Eugene D. Genovese of the University of Rochester; James H. Dormon, Jr., of the University of Southwestern Louisiana; William H. Longton, of the University of Toledo; Charles and Jane Roberts of Sacramento State College; Lester B. Baltimore of Adelphi University; Mary Jo Bratton of East Carolina University; Thomas G. Edwards of Whitman College; and Mr. Peter Friedlander, presently a graduate student at the State University of New York at Binghamton. In addition to cooperation in domestic life, my wife Ellen has made many contributions, too diverse to specify, to the research and writing for this study.

The University of Oregon Research Council assisted me in this study by providing a Summer Faculty Research Grant, and a Younger Humanists award from the National Endowment for the Humanities helped to complete this study as well as begin some others. I am grateful to staff members at many libraries for assistance; those at the Library of Congress, the University of Oregon, the University of North Carolina at Chapel Hill, and Duke University particularly went out of their way to help me. Professor Forrest G. Wood of Fresno State College responded helpfully to an inquiry about source materials. I should like to express appreciation to A. T. Stevens, Jr. and the manager of the Oakridge estate in Nelson County, Virginia, who kindly showed me around the estate.

THE RECONSTRUCTION OF EDWARD A. POLLARD
A Rebel's Conversion to Postbellum Unionism

I.

THE TWO WORLDS
OF EDWARD A. POLLARD

Edward A. Pollard and his intellectual biography have remained curiously unknown to historians quite familiar with his name. Pollard achieved prominence as a Southern controversial writer during the slavery controversy, the War of 1861-65, and the Reconstruction. "Mr. Pollard," the New York *Times* observed in 1869, "was about as well known, to any one at all familiar with the origin and history of the [Confederate] rebellion, as Jeff. Davis or Gen. Lee. . . ."[1] His work has left tangible memorials. His volumes about the Confederacy's history stand conspicuously on library shelves, and a sampling of recent books on the Confederacy will yield many references to him. But scholars have neglected the story of Pollard's development as a contemporary interpreter of the great crisis of the South's history. The available sketches of his life omit some of its highlights and propagate errors.[2] Even their most often-repeated "fact"—that he was the editor of the Richmond *Examiner* from 1861 until 1867—is incorrect. Secondary writers' references to Pollard's opinions are equally misleading; they present a few of his ideas in isolation, torn loose from their places in his general frame of reference and in the process of its development and change.

The course of Pollard's intellectual evolution can tell historians more about the South's course during his lifetime than does any of the particular interpretations he offered. During the political controversy related to slavery, and the Confederacy's struggle for independence, Pollard like many others discovered his Southern homeland's identity as a nationality. He projected a Southern nationalist worldview pivoted on the system of slavery and the values it engendered. After the Confederacy died in 1865, Pollard found himself living in a foreign land—a slaveless, Northern-dominated United States. The experience disturbed him. In time, it deprived him of his Southern nationalist worldview, and converted him to a very different one. He then experimented with justifying the Confederacy on conservative Unionist grounds, to reduce the disso-

[4] *The Reconstruction of Edward A. Pollard*

nance between his old and his new ideology. But the main work of his later years was to consolidate the new order by assimilating former Confederates into it gracefully.

Much of Pollard's external biography is necessarily obscure. He pursued a turbulent lifestyle, marred by episodes of sex and violence. But it is possible, with some difficulty, to learn the principal facts of his personal and literary career. He was born on February 27, 1832, into the distinguished Pollard-Rives family of Virginia.³ He grew up on family plantations—Oakridge, in Nelson County, and Alta Vista, in Albemarle County. He attended Hampden-Sidney College and the University of Virginia between 1847 and 1850, and then studied law at the College of William and Mary for a few weeks until the institution expelled him for misconduct.⁴ He went to California to prospect for gold, and spent the early 1850's in newspaper work there and traveling in eastern Asia.⁵ Returning to the East in 1856, he settled for awhile in Georgia, and wrote occasionally on Caribbean and "Southern Rights" topics.⁶

While traveling through the South Atlantic states in 1858, Pollard wrote the book *Black Diamonds Gathered in the Darkey Homes of the South*, a commentary on the benign features of plantation life and a militant defense of slavery and proslavery politics. Critics immediately accorded it an important place in the controversial literature on slavery, and Pollard achieved the literary fame he had long desired.⁷ He was then living in Washington, D.C., and serving as a clerk of the House Judiciary Committee, but he interrupted that role with a sporadic attempt at law practice in New York.⁸ His first, brief marriage ended in July, 1860, with his wife's death. The grief-stricken husband resolved on a career in the Episcopal ministry, but his zeal cooled during the following winter.⁹ When the first Southern states seceded he remained in Washington, but shortly before the war broke out he threw in his lot with the Confederate cause. He left Washington about the end of April, 1861, and spent awhile in Maryland, perhaps with his brother H. Rives Pollard, the news editor of the Baltimore *Sun*. There he wrote *Letters of the Southern Spy*, an ill-conceived volume of diatribes mostly addressed to President Abraham Lincoln.¹⁰

About the time of the first battle of Manassas, the two Pollard brothers moved to Richmond and joined the staff of the *Examiner*, John Moncure Daniel's maverick Southern Rights newspaper. The

Examiner staff was a wild, brilliant group of pistol-packing firebrands. Pollard, although partly domesticated by marriage to a British lady, engaged in occasional street-fights in Richmond.[11] His role on the paper fluctuated and was less prominent than H. Rives Pollard's. He apparently contributed many drafts of editorials—but Daniel freely rewrote such drafts before publishing them. In the summer of 1862 Pollard took over the editorial page while Daniel was on military duty. Later, his role on the *Examiner* declined and he spent long periods away from Richmond.[12] As important as Pollard's newspaper work was the *Southern History of the War*, which he prepared in annual volumes as the war progressed. At the very beginning Pollard had decided to write a history of the conflict, and his volumes won recognition as the standard contemporary Southern account. By 1864 he found himself widely recognized both at home and in the North.[13] In that year he tried to travel through the Federal blockade to visit Britain, but the Federal navy intercepted him and took him to Boston for imprisonment. He soon obtained release on parole to stay with relatives in Brooklyn, and spent the last part of the year in the Federal encampment at Fortress Monroe, Virginia, awaiting exchange as a prisoner. There, as in Brooklyn, he enjoyed a surprising freedom of movement. Released in January, 1865, he rejoined the *Examiner* staff and wrote *Observations in the North*, a narrative of his eight months there.[14]

After the capture of Richmond Federal authorities imprisoned the Pollard brothers briefly, then released them on parole.[15] Pollard completed his *Southern History of the War*, and promptly planned to devote years to an even more ambitious account of the conflict. Warned of his deficiency as a military writer, he tried to persuade General Robert E. Lee to revise and lend his name to the proposed work's military sections. Erratically, Pollard slipped away to Memphis for the first three months of 1866 as associate editor of the Memphis *Avalanche*, and then prematurely dashed off *The Lost Cause*, the best of his long journalistic histories of the War.[16] Domestic complications pursued him. He had deserted his second wife for another woman, and then left her, too, after a few months. He feared violence from his wife's vengeful friends and relatives.[17] He entered on a very unhappy marriage with a divorcee, Marie Antoinette Nathalie Granier Dowell—marrying her once before, and once after, obtaining a divorce from her predecessor.[18]

[6] *The Reconstruction of Edward A. Pollard*

Pollard's literary career now reached its apex. *The Lost Cause* proved to be his most popular book. He followed it with *Lee and His Lieutenants* and a Confederate anthology called *Echoes from the South*. He helped H. Rives Pollard to begin the *Southern Opinion*, a weekly Richmond paper.[19] Former Confederates, and Unionists too, eagerly read Pollard's histories. But his fame brought him enemies within the "rebel" camp. Some objected to his severe criticisms of the Confederacy's president, Jefferson Davis. But his most bitter critics were military officers, led by North Carolina's General Daniel Harvey Hill. Doubting any civilian's competence to describe battles, they pointed out flaws in Pollard's narratives and reacted vehemently against his aspersions on their competence.[20] Others protested injury to their reputations. In November, 1867, two nephews of Virginia's former governor Henry A. Wise attacked Pollard with gunfire in Baltimore to avenge his criticisms of Wise.[21]

The year 1868—the time of his own intellectual "reconstruction" —was a busy one for Pollard. He moved from Baltimore to New York City. His marriage disintegrated in a series of embarrassing events—two desertions of his wife, suspicions of infidelity, violence and mutual recriminations, and divorce proceedings.[22] Pollard continued his writing without interruption, though, and produced the Reconstruction tract *The Lost Cause Regained*. In September, he published four issues of an abortive personal weekly. In November, friends in the Democratic party obtained a position for him in the New York custom house, but at the end of the year, cowering before Unionist protests about the rebel's appointment, his superiors inveigled him into resigning.[23] The year's worst trauma for him was the murder of his favorite brother H. Rives Pollard, in Richmond, on November 24. Pollard hurried to Richmond to arrange for burial, and he spent most of the winter of 1868-69 unsuccessfully trying to secure the conviction of the apparent murderer—James Grant, a fashionable young man who smarted under the *Southern Opinion*'s insinuations about his sister's elopement. Thwarted by Richmond opinion, Pollard was in the courtroom on March 6, 1869, to hear the verdict of acquittal.[24]

Pollard spent most of the following months with his brother Richard, a drygoods merchant in Lynchburg, Virginia. He wrote his last important book—*The Life of Jefferson Davis, with a Secret History of the Southern Confederacy*. Its public influence, although strong, was mainly limited to confirming anti-Davis prejudices in the minds of many Confederate sympathizers. During the summer Pollard toured the western Virginia springs region for his health, and wrote *The Virginia Tourist*, a guidebook to the area. He made journalistic contacts in Lynchburg, and wrote a pamphlet for publication there.[25]

Although Pollard did not at first intend to settle in Lynchburg, he spent most of his few remaining years in Richard Pollard's household there. He lacked strong roots anywhere else, and he was becoming increasingly incapacitated by albumenaria. Although he continued to travel by rail to other parts of the South, he was settling for the first time into a sedentary life-style. His early religious interest returned, and he joined the Methodist congregation to which Richard belonged. He wrote articles and pamphlets on a great variety of topics, and contributed to the Lynchburg *Republican*.[26] Those later writings drew the usual mixture of favorable and unfavorable criticism, but attracted less attention than his earlier books.

Pollard was only forty when his illness brought his life to an end on December 17, 1872,[27] but he had made his mark on his era. *Black Diamonds* and *The Lost Cause* secured his lasting reputation. His other historical narratives, which had sold well in their time, continued to attract some notice after his death. Scholars were to find the wartime files of the Richmond *Examiner* the most quotable source for an important viewpoint in the Confederacy's politics— and some of them came to credit Pollard with almost everything that appeared on its editorial page. Although the public soon forgot Pollard's pamphlets and articles, his books and editorials have kept his fame alive.

Pollard's intellectual biography offers important insights to students of the nineteenth-century South and the sectional conflict. His career was a protracted essay in interpreting the conflict. Pollard was still a teen-ager in the late 1840's, when the question of slavery in the Western territories began to convulse national politics. The struggle for Southern independence, during which he turned thirty, marked the high point of his journalistic career and provided the subject-matter for most of his books. When he died, at forty, the Reconstruction era was not yet completed. Examining the course of Pollard's thinking can reveal much about the forces acting in the

[8] *The Reconstruction of Edward A. Pollard*

North/South conflict—the slaveholding and "free labor" ways of life, the value systems that accompanied them, and their antagonistic interaction.

Previous historians who have dealt with Pollard have neglected his social philosophy and the chronological development of his ideas. Most have supposed that he stood by a single set of ideas through his adult life.[28] None have recognized his throughgoing conversion, in 1867-68, from a proslavery Southern nationalist framework of ideas to a free-labor Unionist framework. Lacking perspective on Pollard's intellectual biography, historians with one conspicuous exception have not looked to Pollard as a guide to the larger problems of Southern and national history. And the same lack of perspective led the eminent exception—Ulrich B. Phillips—into a serious misinterpretation of Pollard's significance for those problems.

In the 1920's Phillips, then the most eminent student of the South's regional history, identified the "common resolve" of white Southerners to keep blacks in subordination as the "central theme" that made the South's antebellum and postbellum history essentially continuous. As an essential part of his thesis Phillips argued that Southerners before 1865 had defended slavery not as a good in itself, but as a guarantee of "white supremacy" and "racial adjustment." They had been quite conscious, he thought, that racial superiority was their motivating concern.[29] That belief fitted well with Phillips' own white supremacist opinions—but he did not find it easy to document from Southern pro-slavery sources. In fact, the antebellum racist whose ideas he found most appealing was Sidney G. Fisher, who had been not a secessionist but a Northern advocate of "free soil."[30]

But in Pollard's long-forgotten book *The Lost Cause Regained*, Phillips discovered his most valuable Southern source of confirmation. Pollard, he found, had written in 1868 that "the true ground of defence" of slavery had been "as a barrier against a contention and war of races," and that Southerners could regain their "Lost Cause" (white supremacy, not slavery) by forming a conservative alliance in national politics. Phillips took up those statements enthusiastically, arguing that they expressed Pollard's and other secessionists' antebellum feelings. He hailed *The Lost Cause Regained* as Pollard's "most significant book," and made it the cornerstone of his own argument that white supremacy had been the Confederates' rationale for slavery and secession.[31] Subsequent writers have accepted Phillips' interpretation of Pollard's book. One recent defender of the "central theme" idea, for example, has quoted it along with antebellum and Confederate pronouncements as if it were a product of the pre-1865 South.[32]

Phillips greatly misunderstood Pollard and *The Lost Cause Regained*. The volume was, as Phillips wrote, Pollard's most significant book. And Pollard did, in its pages, initiate an interpretation of the South's history that later became popular. But he did not attribute that interpretation to antebellum Southerners. And it did not characterize his own approach to the sectional conflict at any time before 1867 or after 1869. It resulted from a passing phase of his work.

In the context of Pollard's full career, that phase's significance becomes apparent. Until 1867 Pollard was one of the most uncompromising proslavery Southern nationalists. In 1867-68, he underwent a transfer of loyalties that eventually made him one of the most advanced of "reconstructed" Southern conservatives. It was at the point of transition that he tried, in *The Lost Cause Regained*, to reinterpret Southern history so as to bridge the chasm between the Old South and the New. By a sort of falsification of regional memory—constructing for the South a past consistent with post-1865 realities—he anesthetized himself, and his Southern readers, to the impact of their surrender to the new order.

Understanding Pollard's conversion involves understanding his social and cultural milieu—the nineteenth-century South. His conversion was one man's way of making a transition that his entire generation of Southerners had to make to some extent. Pollard and his Southern countrymen came to maturity in one world of relationships and assumptions—but eventually found themselves absorbed into quite a different world.

The nature of Pollard's first world has perplexed many students. One of the most basic questions about the South and the sectional conflict has been, "Was the Old South Different?"[33] The question has two parts: Was "the Old South" different (1) from "the Old North" of antebellum times, and (2) from "the New South" after 1865?

Most students of the question have come to it with a conception of "regionalism" which they derive from twentieth-century American experience. They begin by thinking of "the South" as a category defined by a variety of disparate characteristics: climate, population distribution, speech patterns, eating habits, and so forth. Then, using those indicators, they set out to measure how far the region still differs from "the national norm."[34]

Approaching the question that way, many have found reasons to argue that "the Old South" did not differ conspicuously from the North in the 1840's and 1850's. In many aspects of life, differences within the South, and within the North, were at least as great as differences between the two sections. Northern and Southern whites came from common ethnic origins. The two sections did not contrast in topography, and climatic differences were slighter and had less effect than many have imagined. Agriculture and rural life characterized most of the North as well as the South, and Southern planters depended as heavily on commercial and financial facilities as any group in the nation. Cultural patterns were national or local more often than they were regional. Writers have taken pains to show that such national phenomena as democracy, individualism, manufacturing, revivalism, romanticism, and literary culture existed in the Old South—even if not to the same degree, or in the same forms, as in the North.

But the argument that the Old South was not "different" runs into difficulty when it encounters some of the realities of the 1850's. It does not account for important phenomena, such as slavery and radical individualist movements, that were strictly limited to one section. It is hard put to produce a plausible explanation for the Union's division and the Civil War. It does not explain why contemporaries so generally perceived North and South as "different" and as becoming progressively more different. The political parties' care to balance their national tickets between North and South indicated a general awareness of sectional differences.

The difference was much more perceptible and precise than any sectional difference in the twentieth-century United States. In the 1840's and 1850's, there was little room for doubting whether a particular place (except perhaps Delaware) belonged to "the North" or "the South." New Jersey, people might agree, was not *as* "Northern" as Massachusetts, nor Maryland *as* "Southern" as South Carolina. But almost every American of that generation recognized that Maryland was a Southern state and New Jersey a Northern one, that

Missouri belonged to the South and Illinois to the North. That consensus should show that the sources of "Southernness" before 1865 were much simpler than the multiplicity of variables that defines imprecise "regions" in twentieth-century America.

The great, simple, obvious difference that in antebellum times separated the generally-recognized "Northern" states from the generally-recognized "Southern" states was slavery. The fifteen "Southern" states of 1860 were the fifteen in which slavery was a legal institution; the eighteen "Northern" states were the eighteen that banned it by law. In every Southern state except Delaware, slave labor played a central role in the productive economy. In the South as a whole, slaves were a third of the population; slaves, slaveholders, overseers, and hirers of slaves made up about half the population. But in every Northern state, the early nineteenth century had seen the demise of slavery, indenture, bound apprenticeship, and other forms of "bound" labor. In their place appeared a rapidly-growing economy functioning by "free labor"—the labor power of owners in their own shops or farms, and of wage-earners who hired out their talents by the day or hour. The fundamental contrast between the two systems for organizing society's work overshadowed all other items in regional comparisons. The antebellum United States was a unique experiment: a federal republic composed of states with antithetical labor systems. It was thus, as Abraham Lincoln said in 1858, "a house divided."

The difference born of that basic division extended far beyond the workplace, into social structures, patterns of personal relationships, and moral norms. Historically, the transition from "bound" to "free" labor has been associated with the great economic, social, and cultural changes that transformed the "traditional" ancient and medieval world into the "modern" world of the nineteenth and twentieth centuries. In that change the slaveholding South played the role of a hybrid, neither wholly fish nor wholly fowl.

Although the South partook of many aspects of the liberalization that reshaped Northern society in the early nineteenth century, it remained "traditional" in other respects. Free public school systems became a standard institution in the North, but were almost unknown in the South. Political democratization affected both sections, but South Carolina's government and local government in some other Southern states remained curiously immune. Nowhere in the slave states did efforts to extend participation reach the explosive level of Rhode Island's "Dorr rebellion" or New York's "rent wars." Nowhere in the South did social and cultural ferment duplicate the "burned-over district" of western New York, with its chronic recurrences of popular turmoil, communal experiments, and messianic religious and social movements. Transcendentalism, radical pacifism, feminism, and other reforming "isms"—pushing the principle of individual freedom to its logical conclusion—found fertile soil in Northern culture; but they remained foreign to the South's regional life, supported there by eccentric individuals but not by movements.

The Old South, too, gave birth to a cultural tendency that remained peculiarly its own, in spite of strenuous efforts to propagate it elsewhere. The "Southern Rights" movement preached that slavery was a "positive good," not just a necessary evil or a matter of indifference. The slaveholding system, Southern Rights writers taught, was the correct basis for organizing society, and the "free labor" system, as a norm for society, was unnatural, inhumane, and unstable. Southerners who took slavery as their norm found that it carried implications for almost every aspect of life and thought, negating the "Yankee" ideal of individual freedom at one point after another. George Fitzhugh of Virginia, the most severely consistent proslavery thinker, followed its logic into a wholesale repudiation of liberal capitalism and its fruits. Thousands of others went much of the way with Fitzhugh. Most believers in slavery as a positive good did not at once see a need for separate Southern nationhood. But when they became aware of the full dimensions of the North's commitment to free labor, and the federal government's potential as a weapon in hostile hands, their proslavery convictions bloomed into Southern nationalism.

Twentieth-century scholars, finding it hard to take seriously the advocacy of slavery as a positive good, have tried to "explain" its appearance as an aberration from what they consider "normative" American thought. Some find it hard to imagine that anyone (especially in nineteenth-century America) really did believe in slavery as his norm for "the good society." But is it in fact preposterous to think that members of the planter class, accustomed to the master-slave relationship from infancy, took its legitimacy for granted and incorporated it in their value system? It is more preposterous to as-

assume that everyone, everywhere, has always believed inwardly in "our" moral values; "ours" are fitted to social relationships that few people in past ages could have anticipated. A Southerner of the planter class could see in his way of life unique virtues, the loss of which would impoverish the world's life. And in the North's system he could see much that, by his own standards, was unhealthy and unattractive. Even Harriet Beecher Stowe recognized that her Little Eva could prefer the slave-plantation system—because "it makes so many more round you to love."[35]

Most twentieth-century students, however, find it easier to understand a defense of slavery on some secondary grounds—to protect personal monetary interests or white racial dominance—than one which presents slavery as the normal way to run the world. To explain antebellum Southerners' actions, therefore, they have emphasized the secondary factors instead of attachment to slavery as such or the worldview that followed from that attachment. And the documentary evidence gives the historian some leeway to select the motives he finds most credible, since most Southern writers eclectically combined diverse arguments to defend their system.

But many aspects of Southern spokesmen's ideas and actions are more intelligible by the "positive good" interpretation of the defense of slavery than by any that rests on secondary motives. An opposition to abolition motivated merely by racism or financial interest would logically argue not for perpetuating slavery but for some plan of gradual, compensated emancipation and deportation of the blacks. But in the fifty years during which middle-of-the-road groups proposed versions of that remedy, no significant bloc of slaveholders responded favorably to it. Even in slavery's death-throes, the slaveholders of the border states spurned the generous proposal for compensated emancipation that the Lincoln administration held out in 1862. Aggressive proslavery spokesmen rejected deportation and gradual-emancipation proposals as emphatically as they rejected emancipation by immediate fiat or slave revolt. Their behavior made more sense in terms of positive attachment to slavery than in terms of fear of immediate emancipation's consequences.

Other indications suggest the same conclusion. By 1860 it appeared that economic trends might convert Delaware, Maryland, and Virginia into free, all-white states gradually, painlessly, and profitably. Slaveholders motivated chiefly by greed or Negrophobia might have welcomed the prospect—but the Southern Rights forces in those states regarded it with alarm. A surprising number of Virginians advocated importing more slaves from Africa to forestall the nightmare of a white Virginia. The proslavery spokesmen's behavior lends credence to their claim that they believed in the slaveholding system even apart from its value in dollars and cents and in warding off racial equality.

How many of the Old South's planters, politicians, and journalists took the "positive good" view of slavery? Many of them avowed it, and very few disavowed it. It probably served as a working assumption for many who did not have occasion to use the phrase. It seems a necessary premise for arguments that appeared frequently in editorials and speeches. Apologists for slavery made much of the system's antiquity and ubiquity, its supposed divine origin and supposed moral superiority to the wage system, and traditional theories of social hierarchy. Those arguments implied the "positive good" viewpoint. When the controversies of the 1850s revealed inconsistencies between slavery and liberal democratic values, Southern leaders did not become disillusioned with slavery in consequence. Instead, increasing numbers of them became disillusioned with liberal and democratic ideas.[36] Their attachment to slavery went deeper and was harder to uproot.

The secession crisis of 1860-61 showed most clearly how deep and widespread was the attachment to the system and to Southern Rights. When the election of a Republican president brought the question of slavery's long-term future to the fore, most Southerners who had been sectional "moderates" concluded that they must join the "extremists" in the bid for independence—because they shared the common goal of perpetuating their social system regardless of the cost. Few vocal Southerners mistook Lincoln for John Brown. Most saw in his election only the threat of gradual, indirect pressure to phase out slavery, perhaps with financial compensation and deportation of the freedman.[37] But they staked their lives on resistance to that threat, because it would mean the eventual end of the order to which they belonged. Their proslavery values also caused them to lose faith in Northern conservatives as an effective barrier against antislavery encroachments. Many Northern politicians were willing to apologize for slaveholders on grounds of constitutionality, commercial interest, racism, and expedience. But Southerners had learned, as the Montgomery *Post* editorialized, that only those who

The Two Worlds of Edward A. Pollard [15]

regarded slavery "as we do—as a moral, social, and political blessing" were able to uphold it as well "as we think they should."[38] And advocating slavery as a blessing won no elections in the free states. It was a deep and widespread commitment to the slave-plantation system that made possible the unprecedented unification of the South's leadership in 1860 and 1861. The issue was one of alternative social systems.

The Old South's "differentness" from the North was not of the same nature as twentieth-century American regional differences. The difference between North and South in 1861 rested not on a number of disparate characteristics but on the very organization of societies based on contrasting labor systems. It would be unrealistically one-sided to describe the South before 1861 as deviating from "the national norm." The two patterns of life were developed alternative structures, and until the Northern triumph of 1865 one had as much claim to be normative as the other. That kind of basic social cleavage dwarfs by comparison the present-day regional differences within the United States.

The other half of the persistent question of Southern history is: Was the Old South different from the postbellum "New South"?

As in the earlier comparison with the Old North, many continuities between the Old South and the New are readily apparent. The Confederate armies' surrender did not end Southern "differentness." The individuals who made up the Confederacy's population did not disappear in 1865, nor did all recollection of their past histories. The South has remained the most distinctive region of the United States, and the slowest to adapt to the national norm. Institutions and traditions that characterized the South of 1900—sharecropping, the lien system of credit, race differentiation, political demagogy, and habits of laziness and personal violence—can be traced to antebellum origins. Romanticized memories of the Old South and the Confederacy have continued to appeal to later generations. Although the Radical Republicanism of the Reconstruction years superseded the Old South's politics, by 1877 conservatives of Confederate background had won predominance in every Southern state government. Many, therefore, have described the post-Reconstruction South as a case of "Bourbon" restoration of the antebellum elite.

What, then, had changed since 1861? One can answer: only ev-

[16]   *The Reconstruction of Edward A. Pollard*

erything! Insofar as the South had constituted a distinctive society and culture, plantation slavery had been its source. After the Northern conquest uprooted the Old South's labor system, its traditional way of life could not survive *as a coherent, autonomous social and cultural system.* The characteristics that continued were cogs from the Old South's machinery that eventually found a place in the New South's. But the machines themselves were different, powered by different engines and structured according to different designs. The cogs performed different functions in the new machine, and were refashioned in the crucible of Reconstruction to adapt them to their new purposes and relations. But chattel slavery—the source of the Old South's distinctiveness and the motive power of its drive toward self-determination—had ceased to be.

After Reconstruction, the South usually remained a "conservative" force in American life. That was not surprising, in view of the deciding role that outside forces played in destroying slavery in the South. But postbellum Southern conservatism did not reoccupy the former position of proslavery Southern nationalism. Conquest, emancipation, and Reconstruction had eliminated that ground once and for all. After the conservative politicians unseated the Radicals, the South became a reactionary drag *within* the national order created in the 1860s, but it could no longer constitute a traditionalist *alternative* to the wage-labor system and other national institutions. The South's postbellum backwardness only guaranteed that Northern forces would dominate the nation and would thus largely determine the South's destiny. After 1865 the South degenerated from an autonomous culture-complex to a dependent province. Tobacco Road was a far cry from Swallow Barn, and Cole Blease and James K. Vardaman were not even recognizable caricatures of John C. Calhoun and Jefferson Davis.

In the course of the transformation that accompanied emancipation, a multitude of more specific changes took place. In spite of such retrogressions as debt-peonage, the black freedmen became mobile. They became able to work without immediate supervision, do their own shopping, and live their own personal and community lives during off-hours. Many plantations changed owners and, on most, cultivation of separate plots by tenant families replaced gang labor. The centers of cotton production gravitated from the plantation counties to upland areas of small farms and white population—and the centers of political power followed. The South's cities acquired new prominence as centers of influence and communication, and large cities such as Atlanta and Birmingham sprang up for the first time in the region's interior. The business class wielded much of the social power that had previously belonged to the planters—but wielded it often as agents for Northern interests. The rural South continued to present a striking contrast to Northern cities, but it discovered that it now had much in common with the rural midwest that had taken the Union side in the 1860s. Although the South remained distinctive, it functioned in the national political and economic structure of the gilded age without disrupting the structure's operation. That was "reconstruction" enough to satisfy most conservative Northern businessmen and politicians.

The most effective leaders of the conservative camp in Southern politics not only were unable to turn the clock back; they did not want to. Although proud of their Confederate war records, many of them learned to look back on emancipation as a necessary forward step, assume an adaptive attitude, and ridicule the "abstractionists" who clung to tradition. Worshipping at the shrine of national patriotism and cooperating with Northern leaders, they looked forward to a "New South" of economic diversity and progress. Entrepreneurial models—the trading town, the textile mill, the "scientific" farm—replaced the traditional plantation in their vision of normative society. Ideologically, they were a world removed from the Southern Rights school of thought in which many of them had been educated. Even in championing the shibboleths of "white supremacy" and "states' rights" they testified to the conversion they had experienced—because those concepts belonged to a national conservatism in which Negro slavery and Southern nationalism could have no place.[39]

Writers have correctly described the War of 1861-65 as a revolution.[40] The stakes in the struggle, and the effects of its outcome, set it apart from the customary jockeying of interest groups for benefits within a single system. The War and the consequent Reconstruction propelled the South from the traditional world of bound labor into the liberal capitalist world of "free labor," refashioning the whole structure of established institutions and ideas. The conflict transformed all the contestants—especially the losers—and the arena of struggle as well. Recognizing the crisis of the 1860s as a revolution

[18]   *The Reconstruction of Edward A. Pollard*

challenges the popular supposition that American history has been free from revolutionary conflict over social structure and basic values.[41]

Some will find it hard to think of the struggle of the 1860s as a revolution. Some workers in black liberation struggles, for example, regard racism as a monolithic determinant pervading all of American history, and do not distinguish between different forms of "slavery" (racism). They therefore argue that the emancipation of 1865 made little difference. That viewpoint does suggest the valid points that "free labor" is not a state of absolute freedom, that the capitalism that emerged from the North's victory has been exploitive and often racist, and that it has sometimes infringed even on the limited freedoms that the blacks won in the 1860s. But those points do not warrant a denial of the great change that emancipation brought to the slaves' lives. Millions of blacks spent part of their lives as slaves and part as wage-earners or tenants—and the overwhelming majority of them appear to have found bondage and freedom remarkably different. W. E. B. DuBois warned long ago against overlooking the fundamental differences between systems of class exploitation, such as slavery and wage-labor capitalism.[42] Each has its own character and develops in accordance with its own logic, and the wage system's victory over slavery has been one of the decisive turning points of history. To discount it would distort both the past and the present forms that racism and black struggles have taken.

Other dissenters from the idea that the sectional conflict was a revolution may point to the conservatism of post-Reconstruction Southern leaders. Jonathan Wiener has pointed out that many planter families retained their social power by controlling most productive lands in their counties, and that their political representatives sometimes secured legislation to retard industrialization.[43] Paul M. Gaston has suggested that most postbellum prophets of an industrial "New South" were not innovators but mythmakers. Generally content with the underdeveloped South in which they lived, he argues, they justified the situation by identifying it with the utopian image of "the New South."[44] Such analyses of the postbellum South contain much that is valid, but they do not warrant a denial of the basic social transformation. The power of a wealthy landlord or employer was not that of a slaveholder—as some former planters remembered with regret. The conflict between agricultural and in-

The Two Worlds of Edward A. Pollard   [19]

dustrial interests took place within a common social system. The retarded Southern reality of the 1880s, whose ideologists preached the progressive "New South Creed," was a different society from the slaveholding South whose ideologists had sought to remold the world in accordance with their proslavery values. For all its backwardness, the postbellum South belonged to the world whose intrusion the Old South's defenders had resisted.

The mythmakers of "the New South Creed," as Gaston recognizes, were not the only ones at work in the South in their time. Another school of mythmakers justified the postbellum reality by identifying it with the memory of the overthrown antebellum order. By calming traditionalist disaffection with the new, they did much to assure the region's stability and legitimize its reconstructed but conservative leadership.

If ever a generation of Southerners needed mythmakers, it was the one that survived the Confederacy's downfall. Many of its foremost figures had grown up on plantations, surrounded by their families' slaves, and had imbibed the tenets of Southern Rights in their upbringing. The events of the 1860s crushed their world and set a confusingly different one in its place. They discovered to their consternation that their old assumptions no longer held true. In desperation, they wondered what kind of life might still be possible for them. The recent cataclysm, they found, had torn time itself in two: "before the War" and "since the War" overshadowed all other reference points in their chronology.[45] They had outlived the only world that made sense to them. " . . . [O]ur country is no more," a Georgia woman wrote in 1865, "—merely a heap of ruins and ashes." "I have no country, no flag, no emblems, no public spirit," a lawyer in the same state mourned. " . . . [W]hat can restore that social polity which constituted the Virginia of our pride?", a former official of that state asked several years later.[46] Thousands of others pondered similar questions.

For that generation the question, "Was the Old South Different?", was more than an intellectual exercise. It was the great existential question on which their very identities depended, because the Old South had made them the kind of people they were. They found no simple answer to the question at hand, and they had lost the institutions that had previously enabled them to formulate answers collectively. As citizens of the Old South, stranded on the shores of the

[20] *The Reconstruction of Edward A. Pollard*

new, they had to improvise individual resolutions for their collective identity problem.

The most satisfactory resolution, in some respects, was the one that Edmund Ruffin—said to have fired the first shot against Fort Sumter—chose. After the Confederate forces surrendered at Appomattox, Ruffin draped himself in a Confederate flag, cocked a pistol, and blew out his brains. He, at least, escaped the agonizing contradiction of trying to live as a "Southron" in a world without slavery. But Ruffin's way out, even if satisfactory from an individual viewpoint, was not a practical option for most of his countrymen. The same held true for the projects to emigrate to one of the few remaining slaveholding countries.

Those who continued to live in the United States differed greatly in their personal responses to the Old South's downfall. Some experienced a psychic death when their cause died, or lost their ability to express themselves when their frame of reference fell apart. Others underwent a psychic rebirth into new "American" identities.[47] Some raged more bitterly than ever against the United States and liberal values, living in profound isolation from the world around them. But others joined the new order enthusiastically, openly acknowledging that they had been wrong previously. And still others withdrew into the realm of immediate personal concerns, or compartmentalized their thinking to separate discordant ideas that threatened to tear them apart. Each of those responses helped individuals to adjust their own lives, but they did little for the collective needs of former Confederates as a group.

But some former Confederates ventured a different kind of response that addressed itself to those needs and became very influential. They tried to rationalize or reinterpret their own biographies and their region's, to reconcile their endeavors for the Confederacy with their participation in the order that their conquerors had imposed. They sought to convince themselves and others that their roles in the New South did not deprive them of their heritage from the Old. They therefore made an effort to reinterpret past events, and particularly to smooth over the chasm that the events of 1865 had left in the South's history.

Their approach addressed itself not only to personal and emotional needs, but also to the social and political aims of important groups in the reuniting nation. In the South, former Confederates naturally became the basis for conservative resistance to Radical Republicanism, as they tried to limit the social changes that Reconstruction brought. In building their movement, the postbellum Southern conservatives made use of the cameraderie that united participants in the Confederate struggle—but they functioned as a legitimate force in the new political framework that the Reconstruction Acts had set up. Southern conservatives therefore welcomed an interpretation of the Confederacy that would harmonize it with loyalty in the reconstructed nation. In national politics, too, the conservative elements needed accommodating interpretations of the War. The former Confederates joined with Northern Democrats and other conservative Unionists to build a national coalition against the Republican Reconstruction program. To rationalize their united effort, the former enemies welcomed interpretations that would enable them to respect each other's wartime roles.

To remove the contradiction between the Blue and the Gray—between the attack on slavery and its defense—was a formidable task. It was easiest to do in poetry and patriotic oratory—media that did not require precise definition and rigorous consistency. But it soon entered into retrospective interpretations of the conflict as well. Many participants revised their recollections of the points at issue. The War's magnitude, dwarfing preceding events by comparison, obscured their memories of the controversies that had preceded it. Former Confederates remembered their wartime service with pride, but they ceased to think about the issues that had divided the combatants, and they hedged on whether their side had been absolutely in the right.[48] When they described the Confederates' "cause," they usually confined themselves to the individual soldier's motives for serving—identification with his homeland, protection of his locality, and other factors unrelated to how the conflict had arisen in the first place. The people who thought that way included not only casual wearers of the Gray, who had never inquired deeply into the subject, but also former Southern Rights partisans, who put out of mind the principles they had espoused.

As the Confederacy's memory became entangled in Reconstruction politics, it became a symbol of the chief slogans of postbellum conservatism: "white supremacy" and "constitutional government." It was in those terms, increasingly, that conservative Southern figures defended their participation in the Confederacy. They found some sympathy among their Northern colleagues, for the Northern Democrats believed wholeheartedly in the slogans and even the majority of Republicans did not consider them subversive or illegitimate. They would have reacted quite differently to the doctrine of slavery as a positive good.

Between 1865 and 1900, the harmonizing of the Old South with the postbellum national synthesis became a prominent theme in American popular thinking. In the South, mythmakers gave an aura of legitimacy to the postbellum situation, and obscured some of its features, by presenting it in the Old South's guise. Tradition supplied the mask behind which adaptation took place. Within the conservative leadership, rival interests struggled for power, and each found elements of a usable antebellum past to demonstrate its own legitimacy. Almost anyone could play the game. The Louisiana Lottery Company was clearly an institution of "carpetbag" origin, but in 1877 it enhanced its regional prestige by hiring two of the most prominent Confederate generals to guarantee the legitimacy of its drawings. "The deeper the involvements in commitments to the New Order," C. Vann Woodward has observed, "the louder the protests of loyalty to the Old."[49] Former Confederates thereby glossed over the revolutionary change they had undergone.

In the North as well as the South, most molders of public opinion adopted a "nationalist" consensus when they looked back at the Civil War. They learned to pay homage to the Blue and the Gray together, and built a common patriotic legend on an experience of mutual bloodletting. By 1900, they made that legend a commonplace in the popular histories, novels, and magazines that Northerners and Southerners alike devoured.[50] Most Americans found that they could comfortably identify with the ideals of both the Union and the Confederacy, as the harmonizing interpretations presented them. There was no necessary contradiction, after all, between the national Union and local self-government, or between wage-labor capitalism and Anglo-Saxon racial pride.

The elements that had dropped out of the consensus of patriotic memory were slavery and the Southern nationalist ideology it had engendered. The Americans of 1900 honored the Confederacy—but in terms of their own ethos, not the Old South's. Robert E. Lee and his fellow Confederate warriors found their way into the national tradition, but the proslavery crusade that had set them in motion did not.

The Two Worlds of Edward A. Pollard

The death-throes of the Old South and the birth-pangs of the New were the context of Pollard's life and work. He won fame as an ideologist of proslavery Southern nationalism, and he fostered the Confederate tradition in the years after the Confederacy's downfall. But in his later years he became an early exponent of "the New South creed" of reconciliation and progress. And in *The Lost Cause Regained*, he made one of the first important efforts to remold the memory of the Confederacy and integrate it into postbellum Unionist tradition. His short literary career epitomized the conversion that many Southern thinkers experienced in the transition from the Old South to the New.

II.
THE OLD SOUTH CREED, 1832-1867

Pollard won his literary reputation as a defender of slavery and, later, of a Southern nationalism rooted in slavery as the basis of the South's social structure. Never before 1867 did he conceive of a South, or a Southern "cause," as able to exist apart from servile labor. In the Southern circles in which he moved before 1865, he later recalled, one would no sooner ponder the consequences of all the slaves becoming freemen than the consequences of the sky falling.[1]

It would probably be futile, therefore, to ask when Pollard "became" a believer in the rightness of slavery. He had been born into the planter class in a slave state. His family, as he later boasted, had produced several Southern political leaders and "was connected with the leaders of secession" in Virginia. As a boy, he often heard how his brother John had been killed in a duel by a Northerner whose aspersions on slavery and Southern character he had challenged.[2] Pollard grew up on large plantations, constantly surrounded by planter relatives and slaves.[3] He later attributed his affection for slavery to his childhood experience of master-slave relations. His brother Rives, reared in the same environment, wrote at twenty-two that he himself "ever ha[d] been, a strong, thorough, inflexible pro-slavery man," valuing slavery as "a BLESSING that deserves to be PERPETUATED."[4] Perhaps Edward Pollard could have described himself in the same terms.

Pollard's aggressive defense of slavery did not, though, derive solely from his Southern experience. As a boy, he admitted, he did sometimes doubt the absolute rightness of the world he knew—and he credited the curing of his doubts to his exposure to the free-labor alternative. In California during the Gold Rush, he encountered laissez-faire capitalism in its most competitive form. Participating in that scramble for lucre brought him only frustration, poverty, and loneliness. Even in burying the corpse of his only friend, he had to take care to find a gravesite that other predatory gold-seekers would not soon disturb. He found the dissipation and swindles of urban life in California almost as treacherous as the gold-fields. The uncertainty of the gambling-table became for him the symbol of that part of his career—and, in contrast with it, the security of the Southern plantation attracted him more than ever. He came to see himself as the Prodigal Son: having seen what the world of "freedom" had to offer, he concluded that his father's servants enjoyed a more humane regime. Free labor was not the only alternative system Pollard observed in his travels. He was able also to compare Southern slavery with the other bound-labor systems he saw functioning in eastern Asia, and found it preferable to them as well. He not only accepted slavery as good, but rejected the alternative social systems as evil.[5]

In his early twenties, Pollard probably saw no contradiction between his preference for slavery and American nationalism. The California newspapers for which he wrote took a national Democratic position, criticizing the aggressively proslavery "Chivalry" faction of the party there. By 1855, though, he felt himself an "exile" in California. He contributed to the *Weekly Kansas Herald*, a militantly proslavery paper which his brother Rives edited in the struggle to make Kansas a slave state. That year also found him engaged in newspaper work with William Walker, who was soon to become Central America's "grey-eyed man of destiny." Believing that the true destiny of slavery expansion lay in the Caribbean instead of Kansas, Walker was then planning the expedition that resulted, in 1856, in his seizing the presidency of Nicaragua and trying to reintroduce slavery there. Pollard became a convert to Walker's projects, increasing his enthusiasm as Walker's proslavery purpose became more explicit. In 1856 he addressed a pro-Walker rally in New York City, and a year later he advocated United States intervention in the Caribbean in newspaper articles. The cause of Caribbean expansion provided a channel by which Pollard transferred his energies from American national concerns to the extension of slavery.[6]

During his California years Pollard—like Walker himself—probably did not appreciate the strength of Northern opposition to slavery expansion. But after returning to the East in 1856, he could no longer ignore the political danger that threatened the South's system. In the presidential election of that year, the Republican party, whose purpose was to contain slavery geographically, carried eleven of the sixteen free states. A month later, proslavery extremists at the Southern Commercial Convention at Savannah called for a militant program of struggle for "Southern Rights." Pollard, then living in Georgia, endorsed their demands as the harbinger of a "dawning era in Southern politics," and began to defend the Southern Rights position in newspaper contributions. In the months that followed, he found his convictions growing firmer, and their implications becoming more apparent. In 1857 he was still writing (in a national Democratic paper) about extending "American civilization" into Central America—but a year later, he made it clear that it was "Southern civilization" and a "Southern empire" that he wanted to extend.[7] The experiences of his first twenty-five years had worked together to make him an evangelist for the Old South's way of life.

After assuming that role, Pollard developed an increasingly proslavery political position, which he expounded in *Black Diamonds* in 1858. In that intensely personal document he alternated travelogue and childhood recollections with philosophical and programmatic arguments, for the way he had grown into the Southern Rights movement made those components inseparable for him. His ideas, even about abstract topics, derived from his experience of Southern slaveholding society and drew their sustenance from that soil.

In *Black Diamonds* and subsequent writings, Pollard celebrated slavery as originating the best attainable social system. The essence of the master-slave relationship, as he presented it, was paternalism. It bound masters and slaves together in a hierarchy of mutual "attachment" and associated them in continual "social intercourse." In childhood, they played together—the children of the master class taking the lead as they would in years to come. In adulthood workaday pursuits united them: the master directed his slaves' labor and provided for their needs, recognizing his own dependence on their wellbeing. In old age, the faithful slave became the object of grateful solicitude from successive generations of the master's family. Thus, Pollard explained, the plantation's inhabitants became an extended family of black and white, old and young, joined together in the master-slave relation for their mutual benefit.[8]

As a sensitive alumnus of plantation upbringing who had found the buffetings of competitive life distasteful, Pollard was emotionally attuned to the value of an ordered, hierarchical, communal system. He longed for the security and "belonging" that he had known at Oakridge, his ancestral plantation. Ties of family, tradition, and religious devotion confirmed his attachment. Haunted by a superstitious obsession with death, he felt in the plantation "family" an association so intense that even death could not wholly sever it. He thought often of the burial-places at Oakridge which contained the bodies of his elders, black and white. In the intimacy of his previous fellowship with them, he felt united with them still. His religious hope of future reunion seemed to be a projection of the "attachment" the plantation community had brought about on earth.[9] So Pollard's class identity, emotional needs, and social philosophy converged to reinforce him in his adherence to slavery.

Inherent in his proslavery position was an emphatic rejection of the free-labor system of *"abolition liberty."* He saw that system as an atomistic individualism that tore men loose from the "attachment" that bound labor provided, and set them in conflict with one another. The system of "free competition and demand-and-supply," he wrote, reduced white workers to the barest level of subsistence and would exterminate black ones altogether. The living conditions of British laborers—the misery, for example, of thirty thousand starving street-vendors in London—attested the "free" system's inhumanity. If his black "mammy" had been "consigned to the demon abolitionist," Pollard claimed to believe, "her lean, starved corpse" would eventually have lain "in a pauper's grave." Antislavery people, he thought, could neither feel nor understand the warm personal affection for the slaves that slaveholding instilled in planters. They taught doctrines that gave rise to "licentiousness and discord, and the contentions and parting of brethren." As slavery was the proper cement of society, abolitionism was the acid that would dissolve it into a war of all against all.[10]

Pollard was not defending slavery, therefore, merely as an outer line of defense for white supremacy. He valued it primarily for its inherent merit as the healthiest social system. He believed blacks inferior in some ways to whites, but he did not then see racial equality as a danger to anticipate. He argued that slavery in America had elevated blacks, not degraded them. He expected that abolition would lead not to equality but to their degradation or extinction by the competitive process. Instead of fearing blacks as potential adversaries, he proclaimed that black was beautiful: an unmixed Negro "looked like *home*" to him. His writings did not suggest even a subconscious fear of black militance. He recognized that misguided slaves might rebel. But even the thought of an armed fugitive slave lurking near the master's estate did not seem to frighten him, for he glorified such a runaway as the hero of a story he wrote for his little nephews. With relatively little racial and financial motivation, he defended the system of bondage as in itself a positive good.[11]

For all his attention to incidentals, therefore, Pollard kept slavery and *"abolition liberty"* in view as alternative systems for organizing society, each functioning in accordance with its own internal logic. He tried to distinguish their essential characters from incidental features. He could, therefore, admit as a paternalist that slave auctions were the worst feature of the system, but affirm that the basically benevolent master-slave relationship humanized even the operation of the slave markets. He made a similar distinction in his story about Black Aaron, the fugitive slave. What made Aaron a rebel was not slavery itself but the unnecessary harshness of a Northern overseer who did not understand the techniques of managing slaves. Even while hiding in the woods, Aaron would rescue his master's son from drowning, and he intended to return to service as soon as his master should return home to restrain the overseer. As long as the sytem functioned properly, under the planter's authority, Aaron would function smoothly within it; it was when accidental circumstances interrupted that functioning that he behaved in a dysfunctional way. Like many other participants in the slavery controversy, Pollard was able to evaluate slavery and free labor as alternative general systems that carried with them alternative sets of values and produced quite different social patterns. It was on that basis that he took his stand in the proslavery camp.[12]

Valuing slavery as an inherently good system, Pollard joined zealously in the struggle to perpetuate it. He took alarm when the conservative New Yorker David M. Clarkson, a relative by marriage, suggested to him that economic and political trends might remove slavery from the United States gradually and without social disorder. Pollard rejected the idea of an end to slavery, ever and by any means, as wholly unacceptable. To him, the future of slavery was not a matter of indifference but "a great problem, involving the largest interests of the world." Since slavery was a social blessing, he insisted, it must be preserved by whatever means might prove necessary.[13]

The necessary means, Pollard recognized, would include a variety of measures. He welcomed "reforms" in the system—but only to stabilize and perpetuate it, without undermining the master's authority. He wanted to reduce privileged domestic servants, a dysfunctional element, to "the uniform level of the slave." He warned that Northerners doing business in the South might be secret enemies, and advocated state tariffs against Northern merchandise.[14]

The heart of the problem, though, was political: slavery was "losing *political* ground" within the predominantly-Northern Union, and discriminatory government policies were retarding its growth. Pollard could contemplate disunion and war, if necessary, to save slavery—but he thought the South could still win the security it needed by less drastic means. He summoned Southerners to unite in a solid proslavery bloc, resist the Northern Democrats' siren song of compromise, and demand that the federal government adopt far-reaching policies to guarantee the future of slavery. His program was twofold: First, the government should undertake territorial expansion in Mexico, Central America, and the West Indies, retaining or introducing slavery in the lands it would acquire. Second, it should allow the importation of more slaves from Africa—one of "the greatest measures of social happiness and patriotism"—under cover (if necessary) of distorted interpretations of law. Those policies would facilitate the slaveholding economy's development, give middle-class whites a secure stake in the system, provide for its territorial expansion, and increase the South's representation in Washington. Pollard's program would shock even conservative Northerners, but to him it meant only "Union and conservatism"—because its guarantee of permanent security for slavery was the only condition on which the South could afford to remain in the Union.[15]

In the two years that followed, as the sectional division became more intense, Pollard wondered whether the North ever would concede the necessary guarantee. Many of his fellow slave-trade proponents recognized their proposal as an "impossible" demand whose denial by the North would awaken Southerners to their need for independence. Pollard might hope that, since slavery was right, even Yankees would eventually recognize its value. Increasingly,

[30] *The Reconstruction of Edward A. Pollard*

however, he suspected that Northerners did not respond to the same logic as Southerners. New England's way of life, he concluded, was "barbarous," alien and antagonistic to the South's.[16] Could the South realize the destiny Pollard envisioned for her, if she remained yoked in Union to a "barbarous" enemy?

Abraham Lincoln's election to the presidency in 1860 made the question an urgent one. The states of the lower South seceded and formed the Southern Confederacy. Pollard, unwell and emotionally depressed by his first wife's death, was slow in responding to the crisis. He was certain that the South would suffer "entire subjection and ruin" if it remained "in thraldom to a Black Republican rule!" He despised Virginia's governor, John Letcher, for temporizing in the face of the Republican menace. On the other hand, there were rumors that Northerners might now make major concessions to protect slavery. As a native of the unseceded state of Virginia, who lived in Washington and owned property there, Pollard was not sure it was time to break his ties with the Union.[17]

On April 8, 1861, when he heard that President Lincoln was sending supplies to Fort Sumter, Pollard's hesitation ended. Now that "the cousin of humanity perched in the Executive chair" had begun a Northern war of coercion, he declared, the old Union could never be restored. Condemning Lincoln's war measures as a dictatorial coup, he swore allegiance to the Southern Confederacy. Expecting that the Confederates would soon capture Washington, he stayed there at first and tried to persuade Southern acquaintances to go with the Confederacy. Then he attempted to set up a secessionist weekly paper in Maryland. After that effort failed, he settled in Richmond to serve the South with his pen.[18]

The slaveholding Confederacy's struggle for independence gave Pollard a country embodying his values, and freed his thinking from the contradictions that his vestigial Unionism had imposed. His writing became more coherent and freer from signs of personal neurosis. As a writer for the *Examiner*—the Confederate capital's most extreme Southern Rights organ—he developed his social and political ideas into a thoroughgoing Southern nationalism. He discarded every shred of respect for Northerners and their country. The old Union's history, he contended, had been one of continuous Northern exploitation of the South and aggression against it. Deploring Southerners' slowness in recognizing their peril, he rejoiced that the War had awakened them to the Yankees' "vices and black hearts." "We can never go back," he wrote, "to the embraces of the North. There is blood and leprosy in the touch of our former associate." Describing the Northern effort as "a war of plunder, rapine, and aggression," he insisted that Confederates should never extend the slightest informal courtesy to enemy emissaries. He included in his hostility the Northern privates as well as their officers, and the Democratic opposition as well as the Republican administration, for they belonged to the same corrupt nationality.[19]

". . . [T]he demand for our independence," Pollard therefore declared, "admits of no alternative or compromise." The South should use all necessary means to achieve the goal. Pollard upbraided Jefferson Davis' administration for showing "imbecility of purpose" and making war by "half way measures," and deplored its occasional proffers of peace negotiations. The way to stop Yankee aggression, he preached, was to invade the North, carrying the War to its civilians and damaging their economy. At home, he urged, the Confederacy should use force to suppress Unionists and unreliable elements. Enemy agents, deserters, counterfeiters, stragglers from the army, and blacks who had been behind federal lines should all be put to death summarily. Pollard advocated executing Northern prisoners of war in retaliation for the North's war crimes. He urged his government to purge its officialdom drastically and accelerate conscription for its armies. To win Southern independence, any sacrifice would be acceptable: "It would even be better that the . . . guillotine should be brought into use, as it was in France, when, at the expense of rivers of blood, it gave success to revolution, than that this policy of permitting abuses to drift along . . . should be pursued." Pollard's advocacy of drastic means indicated how high Southern independence stood in the scale of his priorities.[20]

Pollard set only one limit to the ruthlessness of the war effort he demanded: it must not undermine the props of the Southern society it was meant to protect. In spite of his demand for aggressive government action, therefore, he opposed direct martial law as a form of executive despotism. He hesitated to endorse the wartime curtailment of cotton production. Trusting state governments more than the Confederate government, he wanted to put them in charge of administering the conscription system. And even in the Confederacy's last days, he denied that the South yet needed to enlist slaves in its army, much less to free them as a reward for service.[21]

Pollard never lost sight of slavery as the foundation of his country's society and as the underlying issue in the War. Considerably before President Lincoln published the Preliminary Emancipation Proclamation, Pollard announced that the abolition of slavery was the North's war aim. He considered emancipation one of the most heinous Northern war crimes—the ultimate crime, since it was a stab at Southern society's heart. In arguing that the Washington government was a "despotism," he devoted four times as much space to its emancipation policy as to its violations of freedom of speech. The Confederate armies, he once suggested, should retaliate by invading the North to overthrow its social system, dispossessing the capitalists and offering their property to Northern laborers. The revolutionized North, he predicted, would then become a satellite of the South, and slavery would flourish in most Northern states. That scenario appeared possible to Pollard because he thought of slavery, instead of wage-labor capitalism, as the normal system of social organization. For the same reason, he was confident that the North's emancipation effort would not succeed. Black slaves could not function as freemen. Pollard pointed to the South's "God-ordained and heaven-protected" labor system as a prime source of its strength and as the guarantee that its cause must triumph.[22]

He never doubted, therefore, that the Confederacy would win independence. ". . . [A] distinct Southern nationality," he wrote, "is, in spite of whatever may happen, a thing that is obliged to be. . . ." Regardless of the Confederate government's ineptitude, he thought, his people's superiority in "soul" would outweigh the North's material advantages. Southerners would choose death rather than submit to "the horrours of subjugation." Even if the Yankees could overrun the South militarily, they could not truly conquer it if Southerners united firmly in defiance. The cost of suppressing a hostile population would eventually exhaust the North. Whatever might happen, therefore, the South would in the end emerge as a nation, with its social institutions intact.[23]

Pollard's faith in Confederate victory never flagged. His eight-month captivity in the North in 1864 did not discourage him, and when he returned to Richmond early in 1865 he brought yet another message of hope for his Confederate countrymen. He discounted the federal armies' apparent successes as illusory. Those armies, he reported, now consisted mainly of blacks, conscripts, and mercenaries, who lacked ability and dedication. Against such forces, Confederate troops could still win victories—and victories, now, would speedily bring independence. The North's will to conquer was almost spent; everything depended now on the South's will to resist. The greatest danger stemmed from talk in the South about "submission"—voluntary reunion in exchange for Northern "bribes." "There is not a scintilla of hope for the South," Pollard warned, "in any political movement, or in any peace negotiations in the North. It may be subjugation under a disguise, or subjugation by steps, but it is subjugation at last." Giving in, Southerners would suffer limitless horrors; resisting, they would soon triumph. Would his country, Pollard asked, "meanly break down in the last stretch of the course, when the prize and the sanctuary glitter before her eyes and the pursuing tread of mortal foe is behind her?" He was confident that she would not.[24]

The federal army's appearance in Richmond on April 3 came as an unwelcome shock to Pollard. But although it changed the loyalties of thousands of Southerners, it did not affect his. During the first days of the occupation he made himself conspicuous about the city, loudly voicing his defiance of the Yankees. When federal officers had the Pollard brothers arrested on April 8, Pollard continued his verbal protest while guards conducted him to his cell. When he regained freedom a week later, he resumed his tirades in public places, insisting that he would never take the federal oath of allegiance. Rives Pollard immediately announced plans for a newspaper to publish the brothers' seditious opinions, and Edward considered emigrating from the Union he hated.[25]

The North had won the War. It was time, many former Confederates decided, to adjust to Northern Unionism as the philosophy of the ruling powers. But many others, who remained attached to the Old South as their social norm and believed in the rightness of its cause, did not accept Northern military victory as the final verdict. Pollard belonged to that "unreconstructed" group. He resumed, as if uninterrupted, the work he had done during the War: recording the Confederacy's history and propagandizing for its cause. In the latter part of 1865, he completed his annals of the War, prepared them for publication as the two-volume *Southern History of the*

[34] *The Reconstruction of Edward A. Pollard*

War, and laid plans for his more ambitious history of conflict.[26]

Pollard remained as much a Southern nationalist as ever. He concluded the *Southern History* with the unyielding Jefferson Davis' assertation that "the principle for which we contended is bound to reassert itself, though it may be at another time and in another form." The principle, as Pollard defined it, was still proslavery Southern nationalism, and he probably did not expect its future manifestation to differ much from the one that had just gone down in flames. He asked all who had been Confederates to hold fast to Southern Rights doctrines. About the restored Union's politics, he knew little and cared less. He attached to his book only a brief documentary appendix on President Andrew Johnson's reconstruction program. A later edition, appearing during Johnson's 1866 battle with the Republican Congress, omitted even that. Pollard, still a Southern nationalist, described the new president as a "dictator" and his policy as "the programme of subjugation." Johnson's country was not Pollard's, and Pollard's politics had no place in its political spectrum.[27]

In June, 1866, in concluding *The Lost Cause*, Pollard did deviate from his usual course to present a brief analysis of the dispute between Johnson and the Congress. Now that they had "subdued" the South, he wrote, the leaders of "the government at Washington" were dividing into two schools of Unionist policy. He castigated the "Radical" leadership of Congress as revolutionaries overrunning all restraints. The president and "the Conservative party in the North," he recognized, belonged to "an intermediate school of politics" between the Southern Rights and centralist traditions. Pollard had no illusions about the conservative Unionists; he criticized them often in his book. He knew that the "State Rights" they invoked were not the ones secessionists had claimed. He commended Johnson, nevertheless, for his courageous stand against Congress, and found the president's Unionism, which defined in limited terms the changes that federal victory would require, less objectionable than the Radicals'. Pollard suggested to Northern readers that the presidential program was more likely to stabilize a reunited nation than the Congressional. As a former Confederate he "challenge[d]" the conservative Unionists to consolidate victory by making more concessions to the South. Unless the government made such concessions, he warned, a second civil war would probably occur, in "a wider arena" and on "a larger issue" than the first. That was as far as the Southern nationalist Pollard chose to comment on the division within the Unionist camp.[28]

Pollard occupied himself not with politics but with preserving the South's cultural identity. He urged former Confederates to hold on to as much of their old way of life as they could. Approving the intransigence of Jefferson Davis and Henry A. Wise, and rejecting the "submissionist" views of South Carolina's James L. Orr, he called for a "war of ideas" to defend the South's traditions. It would be by far the worst effect of defeat, he wrote, if Southerners should lose their superior "civilization" and their identity as a people. No amount of economic prosperity would be able to compensate for that tragedy. Southerners' primary duty, Pollard told them, was to preserve their Confederate heritage and social distinctiveness, and to concede only minimal compliance to their new rulers.[29]

It was to the "war of ideas" for Southern solidarity, not to national politics, that Pollard devoted his talents in the year after he completed *The Lost Cause*. He compiled *Echoes from the South*, a collection of wartime pronouncements expounding the Confederate cause. He wrote *Lee and His Lieutenants*, a "pantheon" of filiopietistic biographies of Confederate generals. He contributed to the *Southern Opinion*, Rives Pollard's unreconstructed Richmond weekly. That paper—a mirror of the Pollard brothers' interests—consisted chiefly of material glorifying the Confederacy, and secondarily of indiscriminate abuse of Reconstruction and the federal authorities. Pollard took an early lead among those who were founding a cult of veneration for "the Lost Cause."

In that effort he was not writing simply out of nostalgia for the dead past. Still loyal to the orthodox proslavery conception of Southern identity, he was carrying out his strategy of solidifying the South around the Confederacy's memory. He ended each of his books with an injunction to former Confederates to keep the faith. Whatever hope he had for the future centered in them and the Southern Rights ideology, not in any element among the Unionist ruling powers. Convinced of the rightness of Southern nationalism, he hesitated to concede that it was no longer realizable. If he sometimes had doubts on the point,[30] he could reflect that the fluid conditions of the first postbellum years made the future uncertain. Conquest and emancipation were recent events; who could tell whether

[36]   *The Reconstruction of Edward A. Pollard*

they would prove irreversible? "The Lost Cause," Pollard felt, was still a living force, and a renewed Southern nationalist movement might flower from it. He knew that many former Confederates, like himself, had not reconciled themselves to reunion on any terms. They were expressing themselves in the words of Innes Randolph's new poem, "The Good Old Rebel":

> I hates the Yankee nation
> And everything they do;
> I hates the Declaration
> Of Independence, too,
> I hates the "glorious Union"
> Tis dripping with our blood;
> I hates their striped banner
> I fitt it all I could.[31]

Encouraged by that feeling, Pollard urged his readers to retain their Confederate identification and await future opportunities.

Pollard's strategic motive found expression especially in the way he wrote about Jefferson Davis between 1865 and 1867. His hostility to Davis had grown out of his Southern nationalism, since the president had not taken as extreme measures to achieve Confederate victory as Pollard had advocated. After 1865, Pollard used Davis' shortcomings to formulate a plausible Southern nationalist explanation for Confederate defeat. Rejecting Unionist interpretations, he insisted that the Confederate cause had been right, that independence had been attainable, and that white Southerners had almost unanimously sought it in 1861. But President Davis' mismanagement, he argued, had given the enemy undeserved victories, and the Confederate masses had eventually succumbed to defeatism out of disillusionment with their administration—not with their country or its institutions. In his propaganda work for the continuing Southern nationalist cause, therefore, Pollard found it necessary to publish some of his criticisms of Davis.[32]

But his dedication to the continuing cause also moved Pollard to an unusual demonstration of self-discipline. Recognizing that the imprisoned Davis had become an important symbol of the Confederacy, he deliberately restrained his rancor against the man. He balanced his published criticisms with compliments to Davis, and he refrained from publishing his most severe accusations. In 1867, he went out of his way to praise the Confederacy's president as a defiant spokesman for Southern independence and as a figure majestic in captivity. He published five of Davis's writings in *Echoes from the South*, and wrote a laudatory article on Davis as an orator. He appended to the second edition of *The Lost Cause* an unstinting eulogy of Davis written by former congressman William F. Samford of Alabama. Pollard even expressed hope that as an exponent of Southern principles Davis might "yet reappear on the stage of public affairs to instruct and command his countrymen!" The thing that enabled Pollard to suppress his anti-Davis animus was (as he suggested in that statement) his conviction that the Confederate cause had a future as well as a past.[33]

The summer of 1867 found Pollard as firmly wedded to proslavery separatism as ever. He advised Southerners, for the time being, to "say but little" in national politics, and to maintain "an attitude of attentive neutrality" toward "all parties in the North." The task of the hour, he told them, was to promote a Southern cultural consciousness based on the Confederacy's heroic record. The accident of defeat, he insisted, did not tarnish that record. Congress's Reconstruction laws would have little lasting effect in the South if former Confederates would stand firmly in the memory of their wartime struggle. Pollard warned against "the coarse notion . . . that the people should build mills and factories, sum up their philosophy in that great Yankee word, 'material prosperity,' and let *ideas* alone." Instead, he urged, Southerners should "maintain, as far as possible, our peculiar habits of civilization, protect our institutes of honour, reassert the virtues of chivalry, and not forget the exercise of arms."[34]

The last six words were more than rhetorical flourish; Pollard meant them seriously. More explicitly than at any time since 1865, he predicted the resumption of the War. It was, he thought, only "in certain respects, and for a certain time" that the Confederate cause might be "lost." Sure of its rightness, he expected it to arise again. The turmoil of Reconstruction persuaded him that the War was "visibly, necessarily, unconcluded." He looked for the armed conflict for Southern self-determination to resume in the near future. It might take a different form—perhaps a guerilla "war of neighborhoods"—but it would go on until the Confederates won their objective.[35]

[38] *The Reconstruction of Edward A. Pollard*

Pollard thought that black servitude, too, could yet be restored in some form. It was, he still argued, the Negro's normal condition; the experiment of emancipation would fail. He convinced himself that the freedmen were dying out, and that the ones who survived were lapsing into barbarism. Pointing to racist opposition in the North to civil rights measures, he predicted a reaction there against emancipation itself. He hoped, therefore, to see Southern society "re-established on some principles assimilating the happy experience of the former order, and inspired by the yet vital traditions of the past." Somehow, he felt sure, things would return to their normal, antebellum condition.[36]

More than two years after the Confederate surrender, Pollard continued to conceive of the Southern cause and its future in terms of perpetuation of traditional patterns, a war for Southern independence, and restoration of black servitude. Only that conception of it could find a place in the framework of the Southern nationalist worldview that he retained. He had not discarded his general frame of reference when the Confederate armies disbanded. The interpretation of the sectional conflict that he expounded in his postbellum books—particularly in *The Lost Cause*—was the Southern nationalist interpretation that he had formulated in his decade of struggle to defend slavery and traditional Southern society.

The cause of the conflict, according to Pollard's interpretation, went deeper than chance circumstances, and deeper than even slavery taken by itself. The clash resulted from the incompatibility of Northern and Southern societies as two "distinct communities or nations." "The development of America," Pollard wrote, "has been a North and a South; not discordant States, but hostile nations." The sections differed in ancestry, institutions, ideas, and customs; their differences extended "to the very elements of the civilization of each. . . ." Slavery had been the most conspicuous single difference, but the larger target of Northern attack had been "the distinctive civilization of the South," directed by its planter gentry and characterized by refinement, "chivalry," and gentlemanly simplicity.[37]

Although the totality of Southern civilization had given the South its identity, Pollard identified slavery as the civilization's primary source. Northerners, he wrote, had "naturally" regarded slavery as the principal cause of the South's distinctive culture. It was slavery that had "established in the South a peculiar and noble type of civilization." Pollard explicitly traced most of that civilization's major characteristics to the influence of its labor system. Although the tree of Southern civilization had grown to overshadow its original root, he saw, destroying the root would ultimately bring death to the tree. He could hardly find words strong enough, therefore, to condemn the freeing of the slaves. It was, he wrote, a "robbery," an "outrage," a "bold iniquity," "an act of malice," a "crime ... in the name of liberty and humanity," "a holy infatuation, a ruthless persecution, a cruel and shameful device," and "a permanent triumph of fanaticism," "repugnant to all civilization and all morals." Slavery was the life of the South's civilization, and emancipation its murder.[38]

The North's contrasting "civilization," Pollard found, was "coarse and materialistic," characterized by individual acquisitiveness. Northerners, he wrote, were "a people corrupted by a gross material prosperity. . . ." Their ruling elite was "a coarse ostentatious aristocracy that smelt of the trade. . . ." Their animating force was an "unremitting hunt after selfish aggrandizement," often disguised by self-righteous pretenses. Their accomplishments were shrewd business practices, manufactured knicknacks, "prosperous railroads, penny newspapers, showy churches." Their free public schools embodied and disseminated their society's false values. Carrying their "low and selfish utilitarianism" into politics, the Yankees had conceived the evil idea of the sovereignty of the numerical majority, and built on it "a despotism more terrible than that of any single tyrant. . . ." The capitalist elite, out of envy for the Southern gentry that was its natural superior, had launched the campaign of aggression against Southern institutions. It valued the Union, as its savage and mercenary war effort had shown, only "as a source of boundless profit . . . and . . . the means of sectional aggrandizement." Finding Northern business society abominable, Pollard trembled at its plans to develop the conquered South's economy.[39]

Seeing North and South as incompatible societies, Pollard could say little for the Union that had tried to combine them. ". . . [N]othing of political philosophy," he wrote, was "more plainly taught in history than the limited value of the Federal principle." Perhaps the Union had once been a useful convenience, but by the 1830's it had become "the penalty of association of the oppressed with the oppressors. . . ." Patriotic adulation of the Union as such, Pollard claimed, had been a form of mass hysteria infectious only among Yankees. Pollard described the Union's federal Constitution as a "farce," "singularly deficient" for its purpose. Its framers had been ignorant, "silly, visionary, dogmatic, and impracticable," and lacking in common foresight. Their fatal error of basing representation on "the fluctuating basis of *population*" had made the federal government a tool for Northern exploitation of the South. The great John C. Calhoun, limited by his Unionist prejudices, had devised a constitutional theory that reconciled Southern Rights with continuance in the Union—but his model of the Union had existed only in the imagination, not in reality. In 1860 and 1861 the Southern states, belatedly recognizing the Union's true nature, had had the good sense to secede from it. Diverse civilizations could not coexist under the same government.[40]

In fact, Pollard thought, peoples of such contrasting characters needed entirely different kinds of political systems. Unimpressed with "the Washington affair" as a government, he regretted the Confederacy's adoption of "an almost servile copy" of the federal Constitution and an administrative system modeled on the federal one. The South, he thought, should have an original form of government suited to its own society and culture. Pollard looked on the "infamous demagoguism" of contemporary American politics as a reflection of the Northern character in government. During the Lincoln administration, he wrote, the United States had become the kind of government best suited to the Northern spirit—a pure despotism. Concerned only with material things and conditioned to flock after every successive object of public hysteria, Yankees were natural subjects for despotic rule. The Southern character, in contrast, was immune to despotism. The Confederate government, Pollard boasted, had left civil liberties "undiminished and untouched."[41]

Since Northern and Southern values were antithetical, he thought, Southern Rights could never find significant support among the Yankees. The principles of slavery as a positive good and secession as a constitutional right had been "totally unknown" in Northern politics. In the old Union, Northern conservatives had allied with the South only in "a deceitful combination for party purposes." In the 1850's they had betrayed their allies by embracing the "popular

The Old South Creed, 1832-1867 [41]

sovereignty" heresy, a covert device to exclude slavery from the territories. In 1861 almost all of them had gone over to "the worst fanaticism of the North," since they (like all Northerners) considered the Union indivisible. During the War, most of them had protested ineffectively against Lincoln's patently unconstitutional actions, but they had supported his War to suppress the Confederacy. By 1864, they had quietly come to accept even the abolition of slavery. Not even the "Copperhead" extremists had been reliable from the Southern Rights viewpoint; the genuine Northern friends of the Confederacy had been "merely the skeleton of a party," numbered in hundreds. Whenever Northern armies had won victories or the government had cracked down on dissent, the conservative opposition had suddenly vanished—for opportunism was a national trait of Yankees, regardless of political affiliation.[42]

For the Southern nationalist, therefore, Northern politics could produce no acceptable solution. In August, 1867, Pollard or one of his associates stated the case in Rives Pollard's *Southern Opinion*:

> Ours has been a contest between two peoples, not of party opinion between individuals of the same homogeneous population. . . . That was the theory on which we of the South set up an independent government. . . .
>
> It is not, therefore, a case in which there can be a popular reaction [in the North about the essential issues]. England and France were two nations who made war against each other for many, many decades. Was there ever a popular reaction in England in favour of French politicks? Was there ever a popular reaction in France in favour of English politicks? Nor will there ever be in the North a popular reaction in favour of Southern politicks.[43]

Southern politics, to Pollard, still meant the Old South creed: plantation slavery, a uniquely Southern social system and culture, the Calhoun conception of State Rights, and the goal of Southern independence. As long as he adhered to that creed, it would indeed be a waste of his time to look for allies in the North. Of the more than two thousand pages that he wrote between 1865 and 1867, therefore, he devoted only seven to national Reconstruction politics. As a Southern nationalist, he stood outside the frame of reference of Unionist politics. He continued, therefore, to keep aloof from

Northern politicians, conservative as well as Radical, and from their "despotic" government—and to prepare Southerners for a future struggle to restore their pre-1865 society and nationality.

III.

A DISGUISED SURRENDER, 1867-1868

Between the autumn of 1867 and the summer of 1868 Pollard underwent a conversion from a proslavery Southern nationalist worldview to a Unionist and free-labor worldview. He remained bitterly opposed to the Reconstruction politics of the Radical Republicans—but his opposition became that of a conservative within the context of Unionist politics instead of a Southern nationalist outside that context. Pollard did not tell the world that he had moved into a different realm of assumptions, and he probably did not himself realize the nature and extent of the change. In the book that expounded his new position—*The Lost Cause Regained*—he made it appear continuous with the Confederate effort. But the effort to disguise his personal surrender of Southern nationalism did not make it less real. In a sense he claimed that he was carrying on the tradition of the the Old South and the Confederacy. But he was actually "reconstructing" the tradition itself to fit postbellum definitions of American "loyalty."

The destruction of the Confederacy, the freeing of the slaves, and Congressional Reconstruction overthrew the social reality that had engendered Southern nationalist ideas. The overthrow did not kill the ideas directly; as detached notions they continued to live in many minds. But Pollard, and others who continued to live by them, found that they had lost their usefulness as guides to reality. Pollard could not account, in terms of his old frame of reference, for the revolution in national opinion and policy that had occurred in the preceding decade.[1] His course as an unreconstructed rebel was becoming progressively lonelier, harder, and more frustrating. The extreme instability of Pollard's marital and personal relations between 1865 and 1868 testified to the psychological strain the proslavery Confederate experienced after slavery and the Confederacy perished. Remaining steadfast in his old convictions would mean

[44] *The Reconstruction of Edward A. Pollard*

continuing his detachment from the reconstructed nation's affairs. But he had seen masses of former Confederates precede him into the arena of Unionist politics, mostly as conservative partisans of President Johnson. And as Congress reorganized the Southern states on the basis of biracial suffrage, Pollard, like most former Confederates, found himself unable to stay aloof from Reconstruction politics.

The autumn elections of 1867 set him on a new course. Barely two weeks after the *Southern Opinion* writer declared a "reaction" in the North impossible, Northern state elections began to show a conservative trend. Increasing their electoral strength in every state, the Democratic candidates carried Connecticut, New York, New Jersey, Pennsylvania, and California. Many Southerners who had been sunk in despair suddenly took an interest in Northern politics. The *Southern Opinion*, reversing itself, announced that "a general political reaction" was sweeping the North. Reconstruction elections in the South, too, helped to reorient Southern intransigents. In October Pollard's home state of Virginia, predominantly white, elected a large Republican majority to its Reconstruction constitutional convention. The cost of abstention became apparent to former Confederates who until then had boycotted Reconstruction politics. Rives Pollard turned his paper's attention from reminiscences of "the Lost Cause" to partisanship in the national controversy. Edward Pollard was equally frightened by the Virginia election and encouraged by the Northern ones. The turn of political events propelled him into conservative Unionist politics—and, therefore, out of Southern nationalism.[2]

In November, Pollard gave the first indication of his new departure. He announced plans for a biography of Thomas Jefferson—the first book he had attempted on a subject other than the recent slavery conflict. His purpose for the undertaking was to introduce Jefferson's name in the Reconstruction controversy—"to draw from his deeds and doctrines the lessons of to-day; to connect the times of Jefferson and Johnson in the great cause of constitutional liberty. . . ." The project marked an important change in Pollard's thinking. Assuming a neo-Jeffersonian stance, he began to see the conflicts of his time in terms of a party contest about constitutional questions, instead of a war between incompatible social systems. He now regarded President Johnson no longer as "the dictator of the

A Disguised Surrender, 1867-1868   [45]

programme of subjugation," nor even as the lesser evil, but as Jefferson's political heir and the leader of the forces of "constitutional liberty." Previously, Pollard's loyalty to the cause of Southern nationalism had kept him from identifying himself with the conservative Unionists. Now, that barrier was falling.[3]

Pollard did not complete his biography of Jefferson; it probably became a casualty to his marital problems during the subsequent months. He did, however, publish a number of articles that indicated the course of his conversion. He began to extol the American Union in partriotic terms that left no room for his former secessionism. In a series evaluating "The Living Politicians of To-Day," he denounced the Republican party's leaders. However, he praised President Johnson, Secretary of State William H. Seward, and Democratic congressman George H. Pendleton of Ohio—conservative Unionists who had worked to put down the Confederacy. Pollard even reserved judgment about Chief Justice Salmon P. Chase, who had been one of the pioneers of antislavery politics. In selecting "The Living Politicians of To-Day," he did not include anyone who had been a Confederate.[4]

By May, Pollard's intellectual conversion was affecting his view of the past as well as the present. He was referring to secession as a "violent and revolutionary measure." He wrote an article reinterpreting John C: Calhoun, the great Southern Rights statesman, in accordance with conservative Unionist specifications. Calhoun, Pollard claimed, had been a "sound Union man" who had never authorized a state to resist federal authority and had never believed in the right of secession.[5] Pollard's conversion to Unionism was now almost complete.

In the latter part of May, Pollard began writing *The Lost Cause Regained*, a comprehensive statement of the new position he had adopted. After "a prolonged and mature reflection," he announced, he had come to "larger and perhaps better views" of recent events than the ones he had stated in *The Lost Cause*. He described his conclusions as "a novel . . . philosophy on the political question of the day," "a new thought; a new animation for the South; a new prophecy . . . ; a new meditation in the confused strife and turmoil of the day."[6] The book exuded an air of novelty unusual in Pollard's writing. He incorporated into it much material from his recent articles, but almost none from his pre-1867 works. Little of his earlier writing would have fitted the "novel philosophy" he had discovered.

It was the presidential campaign of 1868 that inspired Pollard to write *The Lost Cause Regained*. He apparently began writing it immediately after the Republican National Convention of May 20 and 21, and dashed it off in time to have it appear at the time that the Democratic National Convention met in New York on July 4. Rives Pollard's paper pointed out that the book's "lessons and speculations" were "immediately applicable" to the issues of the presidential campaign. Pollard himself advertised it as a "Democratic campaign document," and reviewers recognized it as one. Throwing off his abstentionism, Pollard was taking the dive into postbellum party politics.[7]

He began the book by settling some scores in the Old South. His initial chapter, on the Confederacy, puzzled readers. It appeared unrelated to the rest of the work—perhaps even contrary to its general thrust.[8] But Pollard took the chapter very seriously. He devoted more than a sixth of his text to it, and wrote it as a fresh account instead of a revision of one of his earlier treatments of the Confederacy. Pollard had his reasons for including the initial chapter, but he did not state them explicitly. He drafted *The Lost Cause Regained* with deliberate subtlety, designing it to be "suggestive"—"to suggest rather than to convey all the thoughts which attach to his subject."[9]

In the "Confederate" chapter Pollard, for the first time since 1865, pulled all the stops in venting his hostility to the Davis administration. President Davis, he charged, had been "blinded by vanity" and "incrusted with the old prejudices he had obtained . . . at Washington," and had shown an "autocratic temper" and a "fatal disposition to repel, as if from . . . rivalry, the company and support of the other leading men of the country." His administration had been an "assured and complete failure" from the start. Pollard even discovered that Davis's speeches, which he had recently praised, had shown "such puerility of mind, . . . such levity and insolence and ignorance all combined, that future sober history will be perplexed to account for them." He found also that Davis's effort early in 1865 to revivify Confederate resistance, which he had then seconded, had only aroused "contempt and pity" for the president "as a deluded man."[10]

Pollard's diatribe against Davis indicated a change in his relation to the Confederate cause. For several years he had restrained himself in writing about Davis, to protect the cause's reputation. But now that he had adopted his "novel philosophy" on the sectional conflict, he threw caution to the winds and blurted out the abuse that he had been withholding from publication. That emotional catharsis had little to do, logically, with the argument of the following chapters. But it showed that Pollard's new outlook had freed him from feeling that he had to apologize for Confederate leaders. No longer would he occupy a niche among the uncritical servitors of the "Lost Cause" cult.

Pollard's critique of Confederate leadership extended far beyond President Davis. He also excoriated Davis's "cabinet of dummies," the "servile" Provisional Congress, and several prominent opponents of the administration. A fatal lack of originality, he wrote, had been a "strong characteristic, running through the whole government of the Southern Confederacy, and pervading all its legislation. . . ." Georgia's Robert Toombs and Virginia's R. M. T. Hunter were almost the only leaders in "the slattern government of the Confederacy" whom Pollard could still commend.[11] His merciless dissection penetrated deeper than the government. He suggested that some Southern regional characteristics—features of the "civilization" he had extolled—had also been liabilities. The South's agricultural economy, the abstractness of its statesmanship, and its disinclination to tolerate hardship had contributed to the Confederacy's undoing.[12] Pollard was serving notice that in taking up the message of "the Lost Cause Regained" he was burning some of his bridges to the South's past.

His bridge-burning became a general conflagration in Chapter II, a scathing history and constitutional critique of the Congressional Reconstruction program. The argument that Pollard presented was the case against Radical Republicanism that conservative Unionists had constructed—and in adopting their argument he adopted its Unionist presuppositions as well. Following the conservative Unionist line, Pollard claimed that President Lincoln had intended a "generous restoration of rights" to the Southern states after the War. That idea contradicted Pollard's previous portrayal of Lincoln as a despot and of Union victory as in itself fatal to the South. In addition, the Confederacy's historian now had only praise for Andrew

Johnson's efforts to smash the Confederacy. He approved all parts of Johnson's reconstruction policy, including the freeing of the slaves and the repudiation of Confederate public debts. He defended Johnson's excluding many Confederates from general amnesty as a measure of "abundant caution" to guarantee that "the governments left behind should not raise a new rebellion" after federal troops departed. He even took care to "acquit" Johnson of the "charge" that he had shown partiality toward the South. Northern public opinion, he thought, had approved Johnson's correct policy in 1865. Those arguments, natural for Johnson's conservative Unionist supporters, sounded incongruous coming from Pollard.[13]

Unionist presuppositions also undergirded Pollard's constitutional argument against Congressional Reconstruction. As his authorities on the Constitution he relied on recent Unionist pronouncements. He rejected the "forfeited rights" theory on the grounds that there was no right of secession; as a legal nullity, he argued, secession could not affect a state's status. He discounted the argument from right of conquest on similar grounds. The Northern victory, he wrote, was not a case of "one government overcoming another," but of "a government merely recovering its own territory and reasserting its authority over its own subjects." He even justified the federal army's occupation of the South, as long as it did not disturb the social structure, as an "affair of police" to "quell insurrection and keep the peace." So completely did Pollard internalize the conservative Unionist line that he habitually referred to "the rebellion" and "the rebel debt" without quotation marks.[14]

Even more remarkable, in view of his previous conception of North and South as incompatible nationalities, was Pollard's attack on the Republican program as disrupting national homogeneity. Republicans, he pointed out, had taught that the Union could not remain divided, half slave and half free. "Is it any more possible," he asked, "to have Negro supremacy in one section and white supremacy in the other?" It was "a great unwritten law of nations," he claimed, "that one race only ought to have political power in the same country. . . ." By giving black majorities control in the South but limiting suffrage to whites in the North, Congress was "drawing a yet deeper line of antagonism through the country." In consequence, "the homogeneousness of the nation is gone; there is no longer a political identity in America." The Reconstruction Acts made another "terrible sacrifice" of national homogeneity in that they applied only to the South—since "the first principle of constitutional liberty" taught that "inequality of laws" was "the prime condition of despotism." Pollard's new devotion to the Union's national homogeneity left no room for the idea of incompatible Northern and Southern "civilizations." Almost every page of *The Lost Cause Regained* implicitly contradicted that primal tenet of Southern nationalism.[15]

Pollard no longer had a quarrel with Unionism as such—only with Republican policies. He took the side of the conservative Unionists, who understood the War as deciding "only the . . . specific questions for which it was invoked," against the Radicals, who considered it "a pervading revolution" that justified "a vital change of polity." The issue was not Union but revolution. The Republican party, Pollard contended, was by nature a revolutionary party. The Reconstruction Acts, which had made "Military rule and Negro supremacy . . . the short definition of 'Reconstruction,'" revealed the dialectic that had guided the party's development from birth. Initially an antislavery party, it had necessarily come to champion centralized government as the instrument it needed to uproot slavery. That fact, not military necessity, accounted for the Lincoln administration's infringements on civil liberties. Under the pretext of a war for the Union the Republicans had also waged a "war against the Constitution." After 1865 they had invented the imaginary "problem of Reconstruction" to excuse their continued use of despotic means to stay in power.[16]

"Despotism" was one component of the Republican revolution; "Negrophilism" was the other. "The black thread of the Negro," Pollard wrote, "has been spun throughout the scheme of Reconstruction." Most Republican leaders, he thought, advocated black suffrage only as a means to perpetuate their party's "despotism." Some, however, were genuine "Negrophilists," to whose diseased minds "the black skin and the most unwholesome peculiarities of the Negro" had become "objects of endearment." Both groups, Pollard argued, were irrevocably committed to the Reconstruction program of military despotism and black suffrage—for only black suffrage could keep the party of despotism in power, and only despotic measures could enforce black suffrage in the South. The momentum of revolution had generated an extreme Radical tendency that was pressing the movement on to its logical conclusion: "general hostility to the Constitution," and black supremacy at least in the South. It did not matter that the Republican leadership had not yet publicly avowed those goals: "a party which prates so much of logical necessities, and preaches the virtue of the *sequitur*, is under especial obligations to follow its doctrines to their legitimate conclusions." The Republican party's history had been a predetermined march to progressively more extreme measures of "Negrophilism" and "despotism."[17]

At that point in his argument, Pollard ushered in the idea of "the Lost Cause Regained." If, as he had argued, Reconstruction events had only made visible the "original concealed wickedness" that had been inherent in the Republican party since its beginning, then those events retrospectively justified "the original opposition to this party"—and thereby vindicated the Southern Confederacy "at least in so far as it was directed against its pretensions." Since Republicanism was necessarily coming to stand for black rule and military despotism, one might, in looking back, conclude that white supremacy and "constitutional liberty" had all along been the real issues of the Confederacy's war against the Lincoln administration. Pollard pointed out that his new view of recent history had important consequences for current politics. It would, he hoped, give former Confederates and conservative Northern Unionists a sense of mutual respect, and provide a program to unite them in an anti-Radical political movement. "The new cause," he wrote, was "the true question of the war revived," and it consisted of "the supremacy of the white race" and "the protection of our ancient fabrics of government."[18]

Pollard did not appeal to Southern testimony to buttress his thesis that white supremacy and "constitutional" liberty had been the essence of the Confederate cause. He deduced it from the Republican programs of 1867 and 1868. To apply the thesis to past events, he had to use adroit footwork and discard Southern Rights ideas. Even then, he did not manage to make it convincing.

In regard to white supremacy, Pollard now thought "that Slavery was a most unimportant object of the war as a matter of property. . . ." Its real value had been "as a barrier against a contention and war of races." He therefore regretted emancipation only "as an introduction to the terrible and greater question of Negro equality . . . ." But from that viewpoint emancipation was only "a small, incomplete event," since "the higher cause of the political supremacy of the white man is *not* lost. Slavery was an outwork of the controversy; but the great battle is yet to be fought." Pollard based his rationale for white supremacy wholly on the claim that blacks were intellectually inferior to whites because of their race. That tenet was now his *"only* defence" for slavery; all his racial policies depended on it. If blacks were not biologically inferior, he conceded, the Radicals' policy of equality would be the only defensible one. Pollard had ceased to value slavery as a good in itself, so he could now excuse it only as an exceptional arrangement warranted by the presence of an inferior race.[19]

That was, for Pollard, a new view of slavery. Racial differences in ability had not been the basis of his earlier proslavery arguments. He had relied, instead, on the paternalistic nature of the relationship, and the superiority of the "Southern civilization" it engendered. He had been so far removed from biological racist theories as to refer to Northern and Southern whites as different in "race." ". . . . [T]he geometrical accuracy of ethnology," he had written in 1865, "is an imperfect and sophistical guide to the truth of history." He had warned that emancipation would endanger black survival, but not that it would endanger white supremacy. Pollard knew that his new position was not in line with antebellum Southern Rights thought. The South's proslavery writers, he admitted, had mostly disregarded the racial-ability question as irrelevant. The Southern mind, Pollard now felt, had "wandered" in a "strange" way. It had argued on "the narrowest and most imperfect grounds"—slavery's benefits as a social system and its constitutional protection—instead of on race as "an impregnable principle of natural law." In his own argument for the black-inferiority theory, Pollard drew nothing from antebellum Southern thought. He simply summarized the teachings of John H. Van Evrie—a Northern Democrat who had been unable before 1861 to sell his ideas to Southern Rights men and who considered them singularly blind to the importance of race. A solely racial argument, defending slavery only as a barrier against black encroachment, had not suited their purposes.[20]

Since Pollard was now concerned only to protect white supremacy, he lost interest in defending slavery as such. He dropped the apologetic habit, which he had learned from Van Evrie in 1864, of denying that the name "slavery" correctly described the Old South's system. He gave up, too, the ideas that the freedmen would die out and that they needed some substitute system of bound labor. He now respected antislavery people who would stop short of enfranchising the blacks. If the freedmen continued as laborers without exercising political power, he wrote, white Southerners would have lost only "so many dollars and cents" from emancipation. Forgotten was his previous devotion to slavery as a system good in itself and as the source of the Old South's civilization.[21] His ability to repress that dissonant memory was a blessing that many Southerners lacked. Long after 1868, some continued to think slavery the only permissible status for blacks.[22] Their position was more faithful than Pollard's to the antebellum South's tradition.

The kind of second-class citizenship Pollard was advocating for blacks was, in fact, a remarkable advance from his previous pro-slavery viewpoint. He feared the black man only in the capacity of "master and ruler, asserting his political individuality, impressing society with his laws, and exhibiting his peculiar nature in acts of authority." It was power—not personal freedom or juridical rights —that he now insisted on denying to blacks. He conceded that they should enjoy the basic "civil" rights of citizens, but not the political rights to vote and hold office. He accepted the civil-rights sections of the Fourteenth Amendment as a "plausible law." He approved of welfare aid to freedmen by strictly non-political channels. He hinted, indeed, that even black suffrage might be compatible with white supremacy in predominantly-white constituencies. "Admit Negro suffrage in the North," he wrote, "and yet the supremacy of the white man is assured there . . . ." He therefore singled out as the "most remarkable" evil of the Reconstruction program not enfranchisement as such, but election practices that yielded black voting majorities in states with white population majorities. Pollard's new racial policies were more moderate than those of most Southern conservatives in 1868. In *The Lost Cause Regained* he adopted the then-rare custom of spelling "Negro" with a capital "N." Van Evrie, who still wanted to restore blacks to servitude, declared after reading the book that Pollard was unsound on the race question. The relatively mild brand of white supremacy that Pollard presented as the essence of the Confederate cause would have amazed the secessionists of 1861.[23]

A Disguised Surrender, 1867-1868 [53]

Pollard also found it hard to read "constitutional liberty" into the Confederate past as a conscious goal. Beyond his claim that later Republican usurpations of power retrospectively made the Confederacy the defender of constitutional liberty, he had to rely on an unverifiable historical dialectic of rebellions. Rebellions, he claimed, invariably underwent a libertarian evolution as they developed. "The lesson of history," he wrote, "is that, for whatever immediate objects rebellions have been kindled, the ultimate fruit, in case of success, is a larger share of public liberty." The American Revolution, he argued, had begun as a simple war of independence, but its success had increased popular liberty in both America and Britain. Behind the Confederate war for independence, similarly, "there might well reside a paramount issue of constitutional liberty" that would have benefited both North and South if the Confederates had won. That argument conveniently relieved Pollard of having to claim that the Confederates had consciously sought "constitutional liberty."[24]

By "constitutional liberty" Pollard meant strict constitutional limits on the power of government, and particularly of Congress.[25] Insofar as that included "State Rights," he could claim for it some continuity with the Southern Rights tradition. But his 1868 conception of "State Rights"—which he shared with Northern conservatives—had nothing to do with the antebellum Southern doctrines of nullification, secession, and extraterritorial protection of the states' institutions. By "State Rights" Pollard now meant only a preference for decentralization: leaving local concerns to local governments. He used a great variety of images to describe the federal system, but they all suggested some kind of "distribution of political power" between central and local governments. The relation between the units need not be static or distant; he thought it desirable "to multiply, to adjust, to interlace the relations between the State and the General Government . . . ." Nor did Pollard see any sacredness in the state as a legal entity; he revived Jefferson's preference for the ward or township as the most reliable protector of the local interest. It was to Jefferson and Johnson, not to Calhoun, that he now looked for guidance on the subject.[26]

The states' rights were only one part of Pollard's concept of "constitutional liberty." The other, to which he devoted more space, was the president's power. Before, he had been a zealous enemy of executive power—but Reconstruction politics made strange bedfellows. Of all forms of "despotism," he now discovered, legislative usurpation was "the most dangerous to liberty, and the most difficult of opposition." He described Congress' effort to curb President Johnson's prerogatives as one of the worst parts of its Reconstruction program, "a revolutionary design upon the cardinal and vital distribution of powers in our system of government." The high point of the Radicals' assault on the Constitution, as he presented it, was not the Reconstruction Acts but the impeachment of the president. Pollard pronounced a large legislature "the very worst depository of unlimited power," and glorified the chief executive as "the constitutional head of the nation," "the source of all political enlightenment" in American government. Solicitude for the executive power had not been a Southern Rights tenet. His principle of maximum constitutional limitation on Congress' power was as far removed from Southern independence as his "white supremacy" was from slavery.[27]

All in all, Pollard's reinterpretation of "the Lost Cause" had little historical validity. Properly speaking, it was not even subject to the test of historical verification. Pollard did not claim that the secessionists in 1861 had recognized white supremacy and constitutional limitations as the objective of their struggle. He said little about those themes in his chapter on the Confederacy. The War, he wrote, had been "only a partial and imperfect exposition" of the issue. "The people of the South," he concluded, "never understood exactly for what they were fighting, and on this subject they received only the most confused instruction from their leaders." The Confederacy had come to grief for want of "a distinct object." Pollard's new interpretation of the cause necessitated that conclusion, for he could not claim that militant Confederates had conceived of it as he now did. The admission did not embarrass him, since contemporary consciousness played hardly any role in his interpretation. ". . . . [N]o nation," he thought, "is expected to measure its patriotic memories by the cold and exact rules of history." What Southerners had thought in 1861 did not matter to him.[28]

But what Northerners thought in 1868 mattered a great deal. Pollard's new program of white supremacy and constitutional limitations, unlike the old program of slavery and Southern nationalism, commanded impressive support in the "loyal" states. For years it had been the definition of "conservative" Unionism. Prominent

Democratic politicians and newspapers based their campaigns against Congressional Reconstruction on their audiences' race prejudices. "There is not to-day a square mile in the United States," the Republican senator Henry Wilson admitted, "where the advocacy of the equal rights and privileges of these colored men has not been and is not now unpopular." Conservative opinions on constitutional limitations also had appeal in the North. Judge Thomas M. Cooley had completed his *Treatise on Constitutional Limitations*, destined to become the most popular law text of the laissez-faire era. The Michigan jurist's views on constitutional restraints, strict construction, legislative power, and local authority closely resembled the ones that Pollard was stating in *The Lost Cause Regained*. Many others cherished them as well.[29]

It was from Northern Democrats and other conservative Unionists, not from Southern nationalism, that Pollard learned the policies he embraced in 1868. He quoted and praised no one as much as Andrew Johnson, his new mentor on "State Rights." He borrowed his theories of race from Van Evrie. He developed the idea of the Republican party's "revolutionary" role from a recent speech by the New York Democrat Samuel J. Tilden. It had been a "Copperhead" Democrat who had first suggested to him in 1864 that the Confederate armies were fighting for Northerners' as well as Southerners' rights. Pollard did not hesitate to admit that the policy he was now adopting had been originated during the War by Unionist Democrats in the North. Supporting the "war for the Union" but opposing the "war against the Constitution," they had tried to confine the war effort to constitutional means and conservative Unionist war aims. The Unionist Democrats, Pollard wrote, had laid the true foundation for postbellum conservative politics. He now preferred them to the Confederate sympathizers in the North, and he took their slogan of 1864, "The Union as it was," as his own slogan for the 1868 election. Their kind of Unionism, not "the Lost Cause," was the source of his policy of white supremacy and constitutional limitations.[30]

What Pollard did in 1868, therefore, was to discard Southern nationalism in favor of the conservative Unionist program of the Northern Democrats. In *The Lost Cause Regained* he tried to construct a platform on which former Confederates and Northern Democrats could unite for the 1868 election. By reinterpreting "the

[56] *The Reconstruction of Edward A. Pollard*

Lost Cause," he tried to give men who had taken opposing sides in the War a feeling of common political heritage. His "Lost Cause Regained" interpretation, he hoped, would help Northern conservatives to see the Confederate effort not as "an odious rebellion," but as "a noble and admirable contest, not unlike that of 1776." It would enable them to include Confederate heroes in their "new Pantheon of patriotic adoration" without compromising their Unionism. They could respect their new Southern allies.[31]

But the readers to whom Pollard's name and his book's title would principally appeal were Southerners loyal to the Confederacy's memory. Many of them still hesitated to join the national conservative coalition. Reconstruction election returns in the South showed that many irreconcilables refused to participate in politics under the new conditions. Many of those who did vote were suspicious of the conservative Unionists. Unreconstructed rebels considered even Johnson's conservative Reconstruction program illegitimate, and castigated him for carrying out Congress' laws. "He did not slay us outright," a former Alabama congressman complained, "but severed the body of liberty joint by joint, torturing us as he proceeded, in his cowardly cruelty, and insulting us by attempting to hold himself up as a martyr for us, and exhorting us to lie still like the eels, and be skinned for his glorification." Southern traditionalists regarded the Democratic party, too, with misgivings. A Southern exile in New York complained because Democratic newspapers there would not editorialize for the rightness of slavery. Some of the Virginians who had been chosen as delegates to the Democratic National Convention were hesitant to participate in the national party's councils.[32] To such traditionalists, Pollard, who until recently had been one of them, addressed the principal message of his book.[33]

He wrote with two audiences in mind. It was to Northerners that he directed his apocalyptic description of the "horrors" of Reconstruction. The South, he told them, was being "daily crucified," its society disorganized, and (with an appeal to Yankee venality) its productive capacity lying waste. ". . . [T]here is a daily terrour in every house;" Pollard wrote, ". . . and in the eyes of desperate men there is a gleam like the flash of swords." Tormented Confederate veterans, he warned, might rise up in violent resistance. Either a "war of races" or a guerilla "war of vengeance" against federal authority might break out at any moment. A year before, Pollard had eagerly welcomed a renewal of hostilities. But now he reversed his attitude. His threats were for Northern consumption only: ". . . we are not advising the South.—We are simply warning the North." He was now acting as a conciliator, not a firebrand.[34]

Turning to his Southern readers, Pollard admonished them against desperate acts. He offset his portrayal of present evils with promises of bliss that would come by patient, nonviolent political action. The lesson for the hour, he told his people, was patience— the greatest of the virtues and "the title to all great and permanent success . . . ." Congress' schemes would be defeated by an enlightened national public opinion, expressing itself at the ballot box. Pollard held President Johnson up to Southerners as an exemplar of patient endurance and faith in the American people's wisdom. From John Milton's *Paradise Regained* he quoted Jesus' decision, instead of using warlike methods,

> By winning words to conquer willing hearts,
> And make persuasion do the work of fear;
> At least to try, and teach the erring soul
> Not wilfully misdoing, but unware
> Misled; the stubborn only to subdue.

His application was obvious: most Northern voters were "Not wilfully misdoing, but unware Misled," and persuasion would win them over. "The American political system," Pollard insisted, "is yet competent to right itself without the violence of arms."[35]

"The True Hope of the South," therefore, was "to enter bravely with new allies and under new auspices the contest for the supremacy of the white man, and . . . the preservation of the dearest political traditions of the country." In other words: to enter the national electoral contest under the Democratic party's auspices. Pollard directed everything in his book to that didactic conclusion. He assured Southerners that the "reaction" in Northern opinion would sweep the conservative forces to victory in the approaching election. The "irresistible sympathy of races" and the traditional American preference for decentralization could not fail to put the Democrats in power.[36]

The "Lost Cause Regained" idea was the rationalization that Pollard offered Southern traditionalists to mollify their suspicion of the national conservative coalition. The South, he told them, had "not lost her cause, but merely developed its former significance." In the current election campaign, she could "repeat what were really the most important issues of the war" and would "have an opportunity to regain her 'lost cause.' " In her armed struggle to uphold slavery she had faced a hostile world—but in the battle for white supremacy she could count on an invincible host of allies outside her borders. Former Confederates might now hope for victory, because Pollard had conveniently redefined victory for them. " 'The South victorious' may yet be the ultimate conclusion . . . ." he promised. "But it will be the victory of the white man; the victory of the Constitution; the victory of law and tradition . . . ." The "Lost Cause Regained" theme was "A Special Consolation" intended to enlist Southerners in the national Democratic campaign but keep them quiescent in other respects. They would be "better able to support the oppression and outrage of their present rulers," Pollard suggested, if they would reflect that Radical excesses were "steadily conducting them to that bar of history where the past 'rebels' are to be proclaimed the true patriots." The "Lost Cause Regained" idea thus served as a sedative to discourage Southerners from extremist action.[37]

By his deft manipulation of the idea Pollard made the two sides in the recent War appear almost indistinguishable. Although he presented conservative Unionism as being, in some mysterious way, the essence of the Confederate cause, he also presented it as the essence of the federal cause. It was the cause of "the Union," against which the Radicals were carrying on "rebellion." It would give the Northern voters "the fruit of the war": the Unionist motive that had attached them to the Republican ticket during the War would now lead them to the Democratic ranks. Pollard's claim that Unionism and secessionism were identical in essence led him into double talk. " 'The Union, as it was,' " he wrote, "is the true and logical expression of that 'Lost Cause' which the country is in prospect of regaining . . . ." The "Lost Cause Regained" idea thus led to a most illogical conclusion—but it was the conclusion that Pollard wanted to reach. The idea suited perfectly his purpose of reconciling former enemies in a common political movement.[38]

Retracting his past condemnation of the Northern Democrats, Pollard urged his readers to support the Democratic party. He argued that its heritage antedating the sectional conflict and its historic advocacy of decentralization made it the natural agent of reconciliation. He did not qualify his endorsement with conditions about candidates or platform. Instead of urging on the party an explicit partisanship for the South, he wanted it to "override all sectional questions," make fidelity to the Constitution its only political test, and give expression to "the patriotism of the country." As he had substituted white supremacy for slavery, and constitutional limitations for Southern nationalism, he also subtly substituted the Democratic party for the Southern Confederacy. He revealed the substitution in a conspicuous mental slip. Quoting antebellum remarks by South Carolina's Senator James H. Hammond on Southern statesmen's accomplishments, Pollard made Hammond's words refer not to the Old South, but to the national Democratic party! A mere Democratic election victory had now become for Pollard the regaining of "the Lost Cause."[39]

Pollard concluded his book with a radiant vision of "The Growth and Greatness of America," completely reversing his previous hostility to the Union. The nation's "very extent," the former secessionist declared, "forbids its division or mutilation. It is a holy unity of art . . . ." Its survival in the War gave national patriotism a new birth and ushered in the "second great era of American history—the era of Re-union." Pollard now joined in the unreasoning patriotism he had previously despised. The Union, he thought, was an object worthy of adoration, and Americans did not appreciate it enough. "The great want of our government," he felt, "is an element of reverence. . . .[P]atriotism must be sentimental, to a degree, to be true patriotism." His own, although of recent origin, fully met the test.[40]

Pollard also gave American government and politics the praise he had previously denied them. Before, he had dismissed the federal system as an anachronism; now, he exalted it as the key to the nation's success and the highest object of patriotic devotion. Before, he had ridiculed President Johnson for ascribing "more than human" wisdom to the Constitution's framers; now, he endorsed the statement in toto. "If the ingenuity of man had been taxed," he wrote, to invent a form of government to suit America's needs in 1868, "the invention could not be more exact than the American Union, as devised in 1787 . . . ." Before, he had condemned the political system as demagogic and catering to "numerical majorities;" now, he praised it for the same reason—its sensitivity to "public opinion." Before, he had found Northern voters subservient to despotism; now, he discovered that their American traits of "extraordinary intelligence" and "native generosity" gave them an instinctive love of liberty. Sure that public opinion, acting through the electoral process, would soon depose Radicalism, Pollard concluded *The Lost Cause Regained* by predicting a glorious future for the restored Union.[41]

In his joyous vision, the triumphant cause of the Union and "the Lost Cause" of the Confederacy fused magically into a single blurred image. Only three years after the hostilities, Pollard was propounding a formula to convert the memory of the Civil War into a bipartisan patriotic legend with white supremacy and constitutional limitations as its unifying ideology. In a sense, the "nationalist" historians and literary figures of the following forty years would follow the trail that he blazed in his conversion from Southern nationalism to conservative Unionism. Pollard did not develop his idea as a systematic historical interpretation; that was not his intention. But he did originate it as a useful social myth, a bridge by which former "rebels" might cross over to loyalty in the reconstructed nation without giving up their self-respect as the toll fee.

Although it served its rationalizing purpose well, the "Lost Cause Regained" idea suggested embarrassing questions about the Confederacy. How—if white Americans were after all one people, instinctively sound on essential issues—could one justify the South's bid for independence? Pollard's Northern Democratic mentors, including even the "Copperhead" Van Evrie, thought the seceders had made "a stupendous blunder." Instead of joining conservative Northerners in political action, Van Evrie complained, they had given up "the government of their country . . . to be blighted and destroyed" by Republican rule. It would be hard for a conservative Unionist to take a less hostile view of secession.[42]

Pollard, in spite of his claim that Republican policy retrospectively vindicated the Confederacy, could not escape the logic of his new position. It was the Republicans' Reconstruction policies, he held, that made their "despotic" and "Negrophilic" tendencies apparent. But even the evils of Reconstruction, he insisted, did not warrant violence or separation. How, then, could he justify the forming of the Confederacy in 1861, when only the extension of slavery (not white supremacy and constitutional limitations) had been directly in peril? Pollard quoted suggestively a remark that his *Examiner* colleague Robert W. Hughes had made in 1861. Before the War, Hughes had said, Southerners had not experienced "hardship and oppression sufficient to justify a rebellion . . . ." Unable to deny the conclusion that logically followed, Pollard suggested that the original reasons for seceding did not determine the Confederate cause's validity.[43]

Basic Confederate policies also appeared irrational from the "Lost Cause Regained" viewpoint. Now that Pollard had given up slavery as his central concern, the thought occurred to him that it would have been "severely logical" for the Confederacy to have freed its slaves and "fought the war on the basis of the emancipation of the Negro." Jefferson Davis, he complained, had been incapable of that "magnificent stroke of genius." But Pollard himself, during the War, would have found such logic and genius completely incomprehensible. He would have recognized the proposal as renouncing the basis of the Confederate cause. Reborn into a new world of assumptions, Pollard the national Democrat already found his Southern nationalist incarnation growing hazy in his memory.[44]

IV.
THE RECONSTRUCTED REBEL, 1868-1872

The implications of the ideas Pollard voiced in *The Lost Cause Regained* went far beyond that book's electioneering purpose.[1] In the remaining four and a half years of his life, Pollard followed the logic of his "novel philosophy" to conclusions increasingly remote from his previous Southern nationalist moorings. The "Lost Cause Regained" idea was neither the starting point nor the end of his transition; it was a halfway house on the road to reunion.

In the latter part of 1868, Pollard threw himself into the Democratic campaign to elect Horatio Seymour as president. He used his short-lived personal weekly, *The Political Pamphlet*, mainly as a campaign sheet. In his effort to win Northern voters for Seymour, he carried his new-found Unionism farther than ever. Instead of condemning the North's victory and the freeing of the slaves, he insisted that Democrats and conservatives deserved much of the credit for them. To appeal to uncommitted voters, he emphasized the depressing effects of Republican policies on the nation's economy as much as Republican racial and constitutional policies. He catered to Northerners' resentment of Southern overrepresentation in the Senate, to turn them against the black voters of the South and the Republicans.[2]

In his campaign writings, Pollard represented his own party as the guardian of the national constitutional tradition against extremism of all kinds. He presented Seymour as a moderate, and recognized that loyalty to tradition need not preclude major reforms. He was embarrassed, therefore, by Southern extremists' pronouncements and by the Georgia legislature's ousting its black members. Southerners' indiscreet actions, he complained, worked "to the great detriment of the Democratic party and its interests in the present campaign." Agitating specific issues, he thought, imperiled the all-important objective of winning the national election. He decided, therefore, that the Democrats should have made "their platform nothing more than an affirmation of the Constitution, instead of a long and elaborate series of over-pronounced opinions on particular questions." Pollard's efforts did not prevent the Republicans from electing General Ulysses S. Grant as president, but they did advance his own acculturation to Unionist politics.[3]

They also put the former "rebel," for a short time, on the federal payroll. It was because Pollard had abandoned Southern nationalism that he sought, and was able with Northern Democrats' help to obtain, an appointment in the New York customs-house. In securing the office he performed the most extraordinary of all his feats of rationalization. The man who in former days had denounced the simple amnesty oath now convinced himself that he could conscientiously swear the "iron clad oath" that he had "not yielded a voluntary support" to the Confederacy or encouraged its war effort. Pollard could take liberties with his Confederate past because he no longer held it as sacred.[4]

The murder of H. Rives Pollard, and Pollard's impassioned effort to convict James Grant, severed still more of his old attachments. The conservative gentry of Richmond, who had come to detest Rives Pollard as a gadfly, generally approved the deed. Many who had witnessed the murder cheered, even though the assassin had fired from ambush and shot his victim in the back. Richmonders issued a warrant for Edward Pollard's arrest before he arrived in the city, and only after great effort did he find a lawyer willing to prosecute Grant. Grant's attorney scoffed at the argument that his client had had a motive to kill Pollard; what Richmonder, he asked, had not had a motive to do so? In his fruitless quest for justice, Edward Pollard encountered more sympathy from Republicans and Northerners than from Richmond's conservative leadership. After that embittering experience, he shook from his feet the dust of the Confederate capital, which he now branded as "the wickedest city of America"—and with the dust went many of his remaining ties to the South's traditional leadership. He was more decided than ever in the new course on which he had embarked in 1868.[5]

The events of 1868 marked the turning point of Pollard's literary career as well as his convictions and loyalties. Before 1868 he had written almost exclusively to defend antebellum Southern society and the Confederacy. At the time that he began writing *The Lost*

Cause Regained, he intended to continue writing mainly on the Confederacy's history.[6] After that, however, he wrote only one book on the subject: his *Life of Jefferson Davis and Secret History of the Southern Confederacy*, which appeared in 1869. In that work he revealed the changes that the "Lost Cause Regained" idea made in his interpretation of history—changes that put an end to his career as a filiopietistic historian of the Confederacy.

Pollard's book on Davis resulted from his changed attitude to the Confederacy. For years, he testified, he had thought of writing such a book—but he had refrained for fear that his censures on Davis, who as the Confederacy's leader was charged with treason, would bring disrespect on the cause itself. It was significant, therefore, that Pollard castigated Davis roundly in *The Lost Cause Regained*. He announced plans for his projected biography in October, 1868—two months before the federal government dropped charges against Davis. He had lost his former solicitude for the Confederacy's reputation. It was a Northern Republican reviewer, seeking Southern testimony to confirm his Northern prejudices, who had invited Pollard to write a "secret history" of behind-the-scenes intrigue in the Confederate government. By responding to the suggestion, Pollard was giving aid and comfort to the Confederacy's enemies. But now that he had transferred his loyalties, that no longer troubled him.[7]

Pollard wrote his "secret history" largely as an expansion of the first chapter of *The Lost Cause Regained*, and he incorporated sections of that book into his text. He reaffirmed in the history the tenets of his "Lost Cause Regained" interpretation. The Confederate cause, he repeated, had been "—rightly understood—a cause of constitutional liberty," of "national" significance. The separation of the sections had been only incidental to the War, and a subsequent reunion might have mended it. Slavery had been "only an inferior object of the contest," and much of the Southern defense of slavery must have been "conventional and constrained, due simply to the resentment of Northern interference . . . ." The doctrine of racial inferiority was the only plausible rationale for slavery. And Republican Reconstruction policies provided "retrospective" justification for Confederate resistance. In the *Life of Jefferson Davis*, Pollard conducted the experiment of writing the Confederacy's history in accordance with his "Lost Cause Regained" idea.[8]

For almost five hundred pages he heaped invective on the Con-

federacy's president. He rehearsed most of his previous criticisms of
Davis—with some inconsistency, since his own views on Confederate policy had undergone changes. But two features of Pollard's
indictment were new. Firstly, he gave partial credence to the very
charges for which some Northerners wanted to "hang Jeff Davis."
Davis had, he claimed, betrayed the Union, he had been responsible
for Northern prisoners' poor nourishment, and he had connived at
sabotage plots to burn down Northern cities. Secondly, now that
Pollard had drastically redefined the Confederate cause, he discovered that Davis was guilty of "misrepresenting" it. Davis' motivation for secession, he wrote, "might have been . . . an interest in
Negro slavery, [or] the eagerness of an old decayed aristocracy to
maintain its insolence . . . " Pollard himself had valued the Confederate cause for similar reasons—but he now attacked them as a
misrepresentation.[9]

Pollard still claimed, at times, to distinguish between Davis and
the Confederacy, and to blame the president for defeat.[10] But his
protestations appeared out of place in the new book, because it
damned not only Davis but the whole Confederate leadership. In it,
Pollard censured almost every important Confederate administrator. The Confederate Congress, he added, had been "remarkable in
the annals of the world for its weakness and ignorance," its "utter
inanity," its "arrant cowardice and mean selfishness," and its "scenes
of personal violence." Many of its measures had disarmed criticism
"by the very excess of their absurdity." Pollard no longer praised
even the Confederacy's military heroes. Even Lee, he now felt, had
shown defects as a strategist, and "Stonewall" Jackson had been a
very uninspiring person. Davis' defects, it appeared, had been only a
small part of the Confederacy's leadership problem.[11]

But the problem went much deeper than the leadership level.
Refusing for once to "gratify the vanity of the South," Pollard told
the "plain truth" that the Southern masses had forfeited victory by
"moral desertion . . . of the cause they had espoused . . . ." Most
Confederate soldiers, he stated, had served only under duress; half
of them had deserted at the first opportunity. Multitudes had evaded
the draft, and disaffection had abounded among the general population. Pollard's readers must have wondered whether there had not
been something radically wrong with the whole Confederate endeavor.[12]

[66] *The Reconstruction of Edward A. Pollard*

Pollard could no longer consistently try to save the South's reputation by placing the blame on Davis. The president, he now admitted, was "in many striking respects a fit and lofty representative" of his nation. Davis had "represented the traditional aristocrat of the South, and illustrated that type of scholarly statesmanship supposed to be nourished by . . . Slavery . . . ." Davis' fatal faults had been defects characteristic of the Old South.[13] Pollard now admitted that the Southern way of life he had previously extolled had proven defective in the War. The Southern character, he decided, had contained much "weakness and inconstancy." The South's agricultural economic base had impeded mobilization. Provincialism had blinded Southerners to the North's resources and determination. The gentry's life-style had rendered it unwilling to make sacrifices. Southerners had lacked political awareness. The South's abstract "statesmanship" had failed the practical test of the war emergency. The "juvenile mind" of the Southern people had made them "deficient in the practical application of means to an end." The Southern exaltation of military glory had led able men to abandon their civil government to Davis' toadies. The "coarse, untravelled people" of the South had excelled in animal bravery, but they had lacked the patience and self-discipline to wage a war of attrition. In short, the vaunted "Southern civilization" had been sick unto death.[14]

Pollard also concluded, under the influence of his new Unionism, that the Confederacy had been conceived in iniquity. In sixty pages that could only give credence to Northern conspiracy accusations, he condemned the Lower South's secession and the founding of the Confederate government. Long before 1860, he reported, there had been a "secession conspiracy" in the South, consisting of the "aristocracy of politicians" who had monopolized federal office there. When Lincoln's election had broken their hammerlock on the federal government, the conspirators had acted to "gratify . . . a mean and slothful greed of office." At the end of 1860 the United States senators from Gulf states, Georgia, and Arkansas had plotted at Washington to have their states join South Carolina in secession. There had been no popular movement to secede. The conspirators, controlling their states politics, had directed the process by telegraph, and had organized the Confederacy at the Montgomery convention.[15]

The South's legitimate grievances, Pollard argued, had not warranted secession. The true statesmen had been the ones who had tried to save the Union by compromise. Having set aside Senators Toombs and Louis Wigfall (two of his former heroes) as plotters, Pollard adopted the moderates John J. Crittenden and Stephen A. Douglas as heroes in their place. In contrast with Davis and his associates, he held up the Unionist Andrew Johnson as the champion of the South's true interest. He pronounced the reluctant secessionist Alexander H. Stephens as good a "state sovereignty" man as the militant William L. Yancey. He pointed to General Lee, instead of Davis, as the "ornament" of the Confederate cause—but he concluded paradoxically that Lee, a Unionist and emancipationist at heart, had never been wholeheartedly committed to the Confederacy. The moderates, he thought, had been right and noble; the secessionists, wrong and treacherous. Now that he was a conservative Unionist, he gravitated naturally to that evaluation.[16]

How, holding that view of the Confederacy's origin, could Pollard keep up his pose as its defender? He replied that Lincoln's act of "coercion" at Fort Sumter had turned "the war of Secession into a war for liberty," and the initially unjustified Southern cause into a just one.[17] Not even that rationalization, however, would make sense within his new frame of reference. About twenty times, Pollard referred to the Southern conspirators as having plotted the War, as well as secession.[18] His confusion on the point was understandable, since from his new Unionist viewpoint, disunion would necessarily bring war. He now castigated the Buchanan administration for permitting the conspirators to act; that undercut his effort to put the onus of initiating hostilities on the "coercionists." In addition, he stated that the plotters had considered armed conflict necessary to achieve their purpose, and that the Montgomery government had taken warlike measures from its beginning. He could not, therefore, make his rationalization that "coercion" legitimated the Confederacy hold water.[19] He had to retreat, therefore, to the ultimate sanctuary—asserting that even if the South had been "immediately impelled" into the War by "a narrow and ambitious conspiracy," it would not affect "the real merit" of the Confederate cause.[20] The only way he could defend the Confederacy in terms of his new values and assumptions was to place its cause on a suprahistorical shelf, beyond the reach of factual verification.

As a matter of fact, the *Davis* book cast grave doubt on the historical validity of his identification of the Confederate cause with "constitutional liberty." In his earlier accounts Pollard had denied that the Confederate government had violated its citizens' rights. But in the new book, he enumerated a host of violations: conscription, impressment, official secrecy, restrictions on the press, martial law, economic regulation, and Davis' "unrepublican style of government" and "feverish fancies of imperialism." He depicted the Confederacy as "a despotism," "an autocracy the most supreme of modern times," "a consolidated government, founded on military principles." Many Southerners, he reported, had felt with reason that the Davis administration's oppressive acts "had extracted all virtue from the cause, and that the war simply remained as a choice of despots, one at Washington and the other at Richmond." Pollard could not expect many readers to accept the military dictatorship he described as the embodiment of "constitutional liberty." Hard put to rationalize the contradiction, he gave up some of his strict constitutionalism of 1868. The War, he wrote, had proven "that in vigorous prosecution of arms, the measures of constitutional organic law . . . must be relaxed . . . ." The Confederacy's actions did not manifest "constitutional liberty."[21]

Pollard found it equally hard to square white supremacy (independently of slavery) with Confederate policy. He recognized that the Confederate slave-enlistment law of 1865, although not explicitly an emancipation measure, was incompatible with his new idea of the solely racial rationale for slavery. "If the Negro was fit to be a soldier," he reasoned, "he was not fit to be a slave." The Confederate Congress' admission of the black man to its army, "side by side with the white man, thrusting him into an unnatural equality," struck him as tantamount to Radical Republican equalitarianism. After confronting his "Lost Cause Regained" interpretation with the hard facts of Confederate history, Pollard concluded that the Confederates had grossly misunderstood the true, invisible objectives of their struggle.[22]

Pollard's attempt, in the *Life of Jefferson Davis*, to write history on the basis of his "Lost Cause Regained" interpretation trapped him in contradictions at every turn. As a Southern nationalist, rooted in the Old South, he had been puzzled by the postbellum world. But now that he was a conservative Unionist, at home in reunited America, he no longer found the Confederacy comprehensible. For the first time, he began to lose interest in the subject. The author of forty-eight sketches of Confederate generals made the discovery that the War had produced hardly any "true heroes." Surveying the "monuments of carnage," he looked "in vain for the intellectual contagion of a great excitement, for those tongues of fire with which men speak in a great war. . . ." The conflict over slavery had not lacked "tongues of fire"; it had inspired multitudes of them. But Pollard in 1869 could no longer appreciate the "intellectual contagion" of Southern nationalism, because its prophets had overlooked what he now pronounced the "true" issues. He tried to put the War out of his mind, and never attempted another chronicle of "the Lost Cause."[23]

The intellectual conversion that ended Pollard's career as a Confederate apologist ushered him into a quite different literary career. In the years that followed he continued to write, producing a steady flow of pamphlets and articles. He published most of that work in nationally-circulated Northern magazines—even, occasionally, in publications reputedly biased against the South.[24] In his post-1868 writings Pollard treated a great variety of topics, but his preeminent concern in them was to integrate the South into the postbellum national structure. He urged former Confederates no longer to resist Northern and Unionist influences, but to embrace them.

Pollard continued to cultivate the national patriotism that he had taken up in 1868. A few months after he completed *The Lost Cause Regained*, he wrote an article honoring his recently deceased brother-in-law, Admiral Henry H. Bell, for his wartime service in the federal navy. Pollard emphasized Bell's devotion, as a Southern Unionist, to the Union. He praised him as the man who had raised the Stars and Stripes over occupied New Orleans in 1862—although in 1866 Pollard had denounced that raising of "the emblem of tyrannical oppression." In his later writings Pollard ceased to scoff at the flag, Independence Day, and the "founding fathers," and instead made them objects of adoration.[25]

Pollard came to rejoice in the North's victory because it had "utterly subdued an element of rebellion that had been accumulating for two generations"—in other words, because it had crushed almost everything in which he had believed before 1867. He found that the "immense display of power made by the Washington government" in winning the War had attached former Confederates emotionally to the nation that had defeated them. "The South," he wrote, "although fallen under the power of that Union, cannot help admiring the power which has conquered so much . . . ." Pollard accepted the fact that the new terms of Union differed from the antebellum ones. The North would dominate the reconstructed nation, and the old Southern idea that the Union was a mere "convenience of the States" would have to go. "The War," Pollard observed, "has changed all this. The Union triumphs, and triumphs as a *nation.*" He whittled down further his conservative Unionist conception of "State Rights." In fact, he came to accept the abolitionist belief that the Declaration of Independence had constitutional force, and gave Congress all powers needed to protect civil rights.[26]

Pollard also modified his view of Congressional Reconstruction. He continued to oppose important features of the policy. But he acknowledged that it was unusually lenient for a dictated peace—much more lenient than Confederates had expected. It did not, he thought, show undue partiality to blacks, and the South's economic recovery disproved conservatives' claims of oppression. The divided populations of the Southern states, he recognized, would present difficulties for any kind of government. He moved toward the center of the political spectrum. The "political revolution" of the 1860s, he argued, had decided forever the paramount questions of slavery and secesson. In the future, he hoped, politics would increasingly focus on more innocuous issues. He advised Southern conservatives to lead the way to the "noble middle ground" of bipartisan moderation. His own program in national politics was a very limited one: honesty in government, local self-government, sectional and racial reconciliation, and general amnesty for former Confederates.[27]

In accordance with his moderate views on policy, Pollard became a less doctrinaire Democrat than he had been in 1868. He decided that President Johnson's advocacy had really worked to Southerners' disadvantage, and he criticized the racism of bellicose Democrats such as Marcus M. "Brick" Pomeroy, whom he had commended in 1868. It was only "measurably and incidentally," he thought, that the Democratic party happened "to be associated with the defence of the South," and Southerners should support it only as "a mere matter of convenience to serve present necessities . . . ."

He thought it a good sign that some respectable white Southerners were declaring themselves moderate Republicans without losing social acceptance. He occasionally complimented President Grant, and he seconded Grant's watchword, "Let us have peace."[28]

In the election year 1872, Pollard based his opposition to "Grantism" on its failure to reunify the country and the suspicions of corruption attaching to it. The alternative he proposed was not a Democratic national ticket, but the Liberal Republican ticket headed by Horace Greeley, the editor of the New York *Tribune*. Although Pollard and Greeley had often exchanged salvos, the former proslavery crusader praised the former antislavery crusader as a great and generous American. Endorsing Greeley immediately after the Liberal Republican convention, Pollard launched an attack on Deomcratic leaders and newspapers that opposed Greeley. His principal targets were the New York *World* and Representative Daniel W. Voorhees of Indiana. Even if the Democrats should nominate someone else, Pollard announced, he would support Greeley on the Liberal Republican ticket. He saw the Greeley movement as "the grand opportunity" for Southern conservatives to unite with blacks and moderate Republicans to form a centrist force in national politics. Since the support of antiadministration Republicans would be crucial to success, he argued, the coalition was right in tailoring its platform to their concerns. Many former Confederates found the Greeley ticket a bitter pill; the irreconcilables would not even taste it. But Pollard gulped it down as if addicted to "Reconstruction."[29]

In society and culture, as well as politics, Pollard now challenged the South's antebellum leadership and traditions. Southern economic growth, he argued, exploded the proslavery warnings about emancipation and the "old political theories" of the secessionists. "The South," he observed approvingly, had "plucked from her breast the dogma and the passion of State Rights," and her "sober and intelligent population" did not follow the "self-constituted leaders" who were trying to excite hostility to emancipation and Reconstruction. The statesmen of "the Lost Cause," he rejoiced, were already "as politically dead in the South as the men of a former generation . . . ." Pollard singled out for attack such prominent Southern irreconcilables as Jefferson Davis, Robert Toombs, and Henry A. Wise. But he commended to his people the advice of the "generous Southern politician" Henry S. Foote of Tennessee, whom he had previously despised as a Republican and an antebellum moderate. The South, he felt, neither could nor should return to her traditional ways.[30]

Pollard asked Southerners to make a massive adjustment to the new order—involving not only "reform in political sentiment" in the South but also "changes . . . at the very foundation of her society . . . ." He raised the slogans of a "New South" and a "New Virginia." The South's "chivalry" must now distinguish itself by leadership in innovation and adaptation. Captivated by "the age of the Submarine Telegraph, the Suez Canal, and the Pacific Railroad," Pollard sought to promote capitalist development of the South. Deploring his people's traditional "want of business talent," he urged them to follow the entrepreneurial way of life that he had previously rejected as Yankee "barbarism." No longer fearing Northern business interests, he advertised to a national readership his native state's channels for investment. In his guidebook *The Virginia Tourist* he invited Northerners to participate in a "social reconstruction" by summering in the Virginia mountains—and investing capital there as well. Mineral springs, he asserted, were an excellent investment that had too long languished in the hands of unenterprising Virginia proprietors. In his guide Pollard also provided information about promising market towns, trade routes, mineral deposits, and fruit orchards. Virginia's resources, he boasted, would enable it to "take the lead of the Southern States in . . . a new era of material prosperity."[31]

The desired influx of capital, he admonished Southerners, was not inevitable. It would depend on their readiness to change. The South, Pollard complained, had "many thousands of lazy white persons . . . loafing on street corners and drinking whisky, perpetually talking of 'enterprise' coming down South—as if said enterprise was something to be brought to them in a box and opened in their midst . . . ." He warned Southerners that some of their traditional mores were obstacles to modernization. Virginia's efforts to attract immigrant settlers had been thwarted, he thought, by Southern business ineptitute, provincial social prejudices, an illusory view of the state's needs, and labor practices left over from the slaveholding era. Pollard told Southerners to emulate the "superior thrift and enterprise" of the North. He advised landowners to divide their estates into small farms and sell them to Northern and foreign settlers. He called for a large-scale program to improve public roads. He hailed, as an impetus to development, the introduction of the free public schools he had previously condemned as a Yankee evil. He now addressed his people as a missionary of the Northern social system that he had rallied them, a decade earlier, to resist.[32]

Free-labor capitalism had replaced the traditional master-slave system as Pollard's norm for society. The change of norms transformed his view of many subjects. In 1870, as he had in 1858, he wrote an essay to justify the inequality of men's economic conditions. In the 1858 essay, holding plantation slavery as his social norm, he had assumed a permanent fixity of conditions, assigned to each class pleasures and pains peculiarly its own, and treated the security of the slave's life as a benefit outweighing many inconveniences. In the 1870 essay, he made no use of those considerations. Regarding a rapidly-developing capitalism as normative, he now appealed to laissez-faire economics, preached the beneficence of industrialization, and depicted entrepreneurial acquisitiveness as the agent of progress. Pollard's vision of the good society and his system of economic morality had undergone a revolution. The Northern labor system had overcome Southern slavery, in his consciousness as well as in American society.[33]

One corollary of his internal transformation was a new view of the social geography of Virginia. Previously, Pollard had combined an aesthetic appreciation of western Virginia with an attachment to the plantation society that had been more characteristic of the eastern counties. After he lost his proslavery norms, he came to see eastern Virginia as decadent and exhausted, unattractive socially and economically as well as aesthetically. Looking through entrepreneurial glasses, he found the potential for development improving the farther west he looked, and culminating in the Appalachian counties of the southwest—"richer in mineral resources than California, and more beautiful and various in its natural scenery than any equal area in America." He observed the same difference in the regions' human resources. Pollard now regarded the leisured planters of the Tidewater, whom he had previously idealized, as effete and sluggish in comparison with the enterprising Germans and Scotch-Irish of the Valley who were freer from "the old social prejudices of Virginia." He also found the humble mountain folk—proud individualists—preferable to he subservient, unaspiring poor whites of the plantation counties. Pollard thus adopted an entrepreneurial social myth to replace the ideal of "Southern civilization" that he had discarded.[34]

His view of the writer's art underwent a similar, but less thorough, change. As a devoted scion of the Old South, Pollard had suffered from the Sir Walter Scott syndrome. He had written his first two books in epistolary form, composing "letters" that were really essays in extravagant language. Even the flowery South Carolina writer Paul Hamilton Hayne had found Pollard's style ridiculously inflated. Later, responding to the pace of wartime journalism, Pollard had outgrown some of his youthful literary habits. Only when he transferred his loyalties in 1868, though, did he begin to adjust his critical taste to a simple, prosaic standard. In studies of American political writing, he then expressed concern that rhetoric should be focused by debate, connected clearly to external realities, and modest in ornamentation. Although he regretted the decline of polical "eloquence," he came to understand it as a natural accompaniment of historical changes that he accepted. He now recognized the pseudo-epistolary form he had once cultivated as an anachronism, an illegitimate attempt to revive a bygone era. To that extent, he participated in the transition from courtly to businesslike style that accompanied the Northern middle class' victory over the planter aristocracy.[35]

Pollard's ongoing intellectual "reconstruction" changed his opinions on race as much as on other subjects. Only in the transitional phase of 1868 did he express emotional antipathy to blacks and suggest colonizing them in Africa. In the years that followed, he regarded them more favorably. They were not degenerating, he saw, but advancing—working hard, building stable institutions, and showing an initiative of which slaveholders had not believed them capable. Except for the habit of pilfering which slavery had inculcated, they were no more inclined to crime or vice than whites were. They seemed, Pollard thought, to have an inborn talent for public speaking. Slaveholders, he now realized, had been blind to the blacks' abilities, and the idea that blacks could not prosper as freemen was a "lost theory" that would have to die with "the Lost Cause." Pollard's enthusiastic view of the freedmen surprised Northern editors, and drew from his former associate George W. Bagby the sneer that Pollard's article on "The Romance of the Negro" was indeed pure romance.[36]

As he gained respect for blacks, Pollard took a more enlightened view of their civil rights. Reexamining the Reconstruction civil rights laws, he found them equitable and inoffensive. Applying only in cases in which law provided a rule of action, he argued, they did not impose "social equality." A future law to desegregate public accommodations, he warned, would contribute to racial friction. But self-respecting Southern gentlefolk, he thought, should not feel degraded by sitting beside blacks on trains or in meeting-halls. Pollard advocated separate-but-equal schools, where practicable, as the most convenient system—but for overwhelmingly-white communities he approved of integration as the only way to equalize facilities. Black suffrage, too, ceased to irritate him. He now saw enfranchisement as a necessary concomitant of emancipation: the freedmen needed to vote to protect their other rights. Although he had reservations about universal suffrage, he rejected race as a suffrage qualification. The blacks, he observed, were voting honestly and intelligently. For the 1869 Virginia election, he wrote a conservative pamphlet addressed to black voters.[37]

Pollard's racial enlightenment did not stop at passive acceptance of blacks' rights. He protested against the Negrophobia that other Southern conservatives manifested. The Black Codes of 1865, he declared, had been "infamous to the last degree." Anti-Negro bias, he complained, pervaded the conversation and writings of Southern whites; blacks were subject to continual abuse, and whites denied them fair wages and equal justice. Pollard called for reform, urging landowners to pay higher wages and enable their black farmhands to acquire farms of their own. While most Southern conservatives were conveniently ignoring Ku Klux Klan atrocities, he denounced the Klan as "one of the vilest demonstrations of lynch law," impelled by cowardice and "the lowest passions" to persecute "the most helpless" groups in the population. Although he still opposed federal military intervention, he called for vigorous civil action to have the Klans "ruthlessly hunted down, and exterminated without compunction and without mercy." He believed that the punishments in federal anti-Klan actions had been, if anything, too lenient. Although Pollard claimed that the direct perpetrators of racist violence were poor whites, he argued that community leaders deserved much of the blame for it. Their racist utterances and political appeals encouraged the violence, he charged, and they neglected to suppress it with their local resources. Southern conservatives, he insisted, were guilty of gross racial injustice.[38]

Pollard had not ceased to be a white supremacist. He did not believe blacks were fully equal to whites in intellect, and he did not intend to give them their full proportion of social power. He pointed out to freedmen their economic dependence on whites, advised them to take a gradualist approach, and warned them against independent political action and commitment to Republicanism. But he admired them as "a strange poetic race" that was making great strides in spite of outrageous impositions. Believing that "the cause of the black man" was invested with *"the great colours of history,"* he vowed to become a "champion" of their rights. Pollard hoped to forge an alliance between blacks and white conservatives, by inducing the more enlightened conservatives to assist the freedmen and actively uphold their rights. Recognizing the Negrophobic conservative as "a dirty enemy," Pollard tried to persuade blacks that an enlightened conservative would be a more valuable ally than a Republican. Pollard's argument on that point was not persuasive, and his approach to blacks was a condescending one. He had become, however, one of the most advanced Southern conservatives of his day.[39]

As Pollard cast off his ideological ties to the Old South, he became more critical in appraising his region's past. He made fun of some traditional Virginia legends, described the white colonists' brutal treatment of Indians, and deprecated such regional heroes as Jefferson, Patrick Henry, and Calhoun. Slavery, he now recognized, had denied blacks the freedom they deserved, "oppressed" white nonslaveholders, and brought about the Civil War. Statesmanship, he decided, had become a "lost art" in the South as early as the 1830s. He rejected the theory of secession as well as the practice. The only legitimate way, he decided, that Southerners might have sought independence would have been to apply to the North for division of the Union by common consent. He stopped holding Unionists' roles in the War against them, and he admitted that the two sides had shown about equal cruelty in waging it. The Confederate leaders, he thought, had erred in 1864 when they spurned feelers for negotiated reunion. President Davis should have resigned his office, accepting reunion and emancipation, before the Confederacy collapsed militarily. Pollard's metamorphosis thus brought Pollard from one extreme to the other in his rationale for reproaching Davis. In 1862, he condemned Davis for lack of aggressiveness in resisting the North; in 1872, he condemned him for persistence in resisting at all. Pollard no longer idealized the Old South and the Confederacy.[40]

As Pollard emancipated himself from the Old South's hold on him, he lost interest in the "Lost Cause Regained" idea that he had devised in 1868. He had used the "special consolation" as a crutch, to make his transition from one frame of reference to another less traumatic. After he completed the transition, he ceased to need the crutch—so he set it aside. He began to refer to "the Lost Cause" as lost indeed. He denied Republican accusations that " 'Conservatives' is but another word for 'Confederates,' " and that Southerners wanted to "attempt to regain 'the Lost Cause' "—renouncing in effect his 1868 rationalization.[41]

Pollard did not wholly discard, though, his desire to harmonize his region's past with his new loyalties. His 1868 article on Calhoun was his first effort in that direction, the *The Lost Cause Regained* was his most significant. But they were not the only ones. In 1871 Pollard tried to read his post-1869 attitude to blacks back into his antebellum proslavery book *Black Diamonds*. In 1872 he referred to the proposal in early 1865 that the Confederates surrender independence and slavery as embodying "the last hopes of the Southern Confederacy." The contradiction in terms evidenced a lingering trace of the "Lost Cause Regained" idea, which conceptualized the Confederate cause as divorced from independence and slavery. Those hints in his later writing suggested that Pollard would still like, somehow, to bridge the gap between the slaveholding past and the slaveless present.[42]

Shortly before his death he made a final effort to do so in an article on "The Anti-Slavery Men of the South." Slavery, he decided, had been good in that it acculturated Africans in western society, but bad in that it sanctioned cruel treatment. There had been, he claimed, a movement in the South to correct the system's abuses; the enlightened planters of the Revolutionary era had been America's first "anti-slavery men." Their criticisms had been the visible indication of a division—"in some measure . . . unconscious and undeveloped"—about slavery in Southern opinion. Most slaveholders, Pollard liked to think, would have accepted compensated emancipation. But the Southern "anti-slavery men," fearing racial conflict, had advocated reform of slave codes instead of emancipation. Before long, alarmed by the abolitionists' extremism, they had beaten a "weak and misjudged" retreat. "Reform" had been a wise policy in its day, Pollard thought—but by 1860 slavery had completed its historic mission, and its continuance would have been "an unpardonable oppression . . . that would have . . . dragged to the dust the very vitals of the South." So it had perished, providentially, at exactly the right time![43]

Pollard presented that tortured argument, like its "Lost Cause Regained" predecessor, as an historical rationalization for his reconciliation projects. He tailored it to justify everyone in the reconstructed Union: slavery's defenders had been right in the beginning although wrong in the end, and its opponents right in the end although wrong in the beginning. In addition, the argument entitled every Southerner (including Pollard) who had ever thought of "reforming" slavery to claim to have been an "anti-slavery man." It also gave Pollard a precedent to invoke when he asked Southern conservatives to act liberally toward blacks. 'The Anti-Slavery Men of the South" was a fitting conclusion to the Unionist phase of Pollard's career, which had begun with the Calhoun article and *The Lost Cause Regained*.[44]

By the time that Pollard died, at the end of 1872, the implications of the "novel philosophy" he had adopted in 1868 had made him a model of the "reconstructed" former Confederate. *Appleton's Annual Cyclopedia* perceptively summarized the work of his later years:

> He had abated much of his old rancor . . . and was evidently convinced that the South could best recover her lost prestige, by the general diffusion of education, and the development of her great industrial advantages. He had, indeed, for three or four years before his death, advocated very heartily a recognition of the national authority in the South, and had warmly supported the Liberal movement and its candidates.

The erstwhile "rebel" had come a long way indeed.[45]

Pollard's relatives interred his body, as he had wished, in the Oakridge plantation cemetery, next to Rives Pollard's grave. The estate had passed out of the family in 1865—sold by Pollard's uncle Alexander Rives, a Republican whom President Grant had appointed as a federal judge. The cemetery remained, though, to receive its last Pollard corpse. Near the new, unmarked grave stood stately gravestones commemorating the generations of Oakridge planters who had lived out their lives in the world of masters and slaves.[46] Pollard had grown up in that world, and had belonged to it. But he had lived to see the downfall of the order that once had seemed as permanent and natural as the fields and hills, as the progression of seedtime and harvest. The world of masters and slaves had passed away; Oakridge and the South now belonged to the world of employers and wage-earners, of landlords and tenants. So did Pollard, by the time his bones were laid beside those of his planter forbears. He had made himself at home in the brave new world of free-labor capitalism, as a thoroughly naturalized citizen of the reconstructed Union.

V.

CONCLUSIONS AND IMPLICATIONS

Pollard and his writings do not fit easily into historical interpretations that minimize the slaveholding South's "differentness" and the changes that resulted from its downfall. Ulrich B. Phillips did appeal to *The Lost Cause Regained* to support such an interpretation. He sought assurance that the institutions and ideas normative to Southerners of his time rested on an unshaken historical continuity and an unshakable social consensus. Looking back from the 1920's, he found in Pollard's text statements that buttressed his beliefs about "The Central Theme of Southern History."

But the full story of Pollard and his book does not support Phillips' theory; indeed, it casts doubt on it. Pollard did not claim that Southern secessionists had seen their cause as a mere "white supremacy," or had been indifferent to slavery as such. The program that he himself derived from the South's antebellum situation was proslavery Southern nationalism. If his first loyalty was not to slavery as such, it was to the "Southern civilization" whose necessary substructure was slavery. The allegiance that the slaveholding South instilled in him was so tenacious that he adhered to it for two and a half years after the Confederacy fell.

After Pollard gave up his proslavery position, he did profess the "Lost Cause Regained" idea for a time, to rationalize his conversion to conservative Unionism. He had little success, though, in making that idea intellectually persuasive; its contradictions were too much for him. And in the years that followed, the logic of his new Unionism led him to repudiate more and more of the South's antebellum traditions. He had hoped to harmonize the Old South and the New—but in fact his commitment to the New led to the progressive exclusion of the Old.

The theme that dominated Pollard's story from beginning to end was the "irrepressible conflict" between the sectional "civilizations" —between plantation slavery and wage-labor capitalism, between

Conclusions and Implications [81]

Southern separatism and Northern Unionism. In 1868, Pollard went over from the losing side to the winning one. But that should not lend support to efforts to rationalize the conflict out of existence.

The Lost Cause Regained, which was the principal primary source Phillips cited to support his "Central Theme" thesis, gives it no real support. In spite of Phillips' effort, the downfall of slavery offers more to the study of social revolution than to that of social continuity. "The people of the South," C. Vann Woodward has remarked, "should be the last Americans to expect indefinite continuity of their institutions and social arrangements."[1] Pollard's intellectual biography lends more credence to that assertion than to Phillips' claim of continuity.

The history of ideas concerns itself not only with particular ideas, but also with the general structures of norms, values, and assumptions that provide groups their basic equipment for understanding and interacting with their world. The German word *Weltanschauung*, or worldview, has served as the most convenient term to describe such a general structure.

The proslavery traditionalism of Pollard's early days and the progressive Unionism he later espoused were alternative worldviews, stemming from postulates instilled by alternative social systems. They embodied contrasting values and contrasting norms for society and culture. Fully to internalize one as one's worldview would necessarily exclude the other from that role. Both were rooted in "the real world"—but in different real worlds. The one belonged to the slaveholding society of the antebellum South; the other, to the free-labor society of the antebellum North and the postbellum nation.

The Old South Creed was not, as some have argued, an air-castle detached from reality. In the context of the society to which it belonged, it served as a reliable guide to reality. It enabled the Southern Rights school, who internalized it most completely, to anticipate the events of the 1850's much better than their moderate critics could. But it did not enable them to foresee the devastating defeat that their system suffered in the War. And after the North conquered and the slaves went free, it could offer no significant guidance. Then, with its social foundations cut away, it became in truth an air-castle. After that, the only Southerners who could comfortably retain it in its entirety were those who could isolate themselves most completely from the world around them. Mrs. Blake, the blind matriarch of Ellen Glasgow's novel *The Deliverance*, might serve as their prototype. Mrs. Blake's relatives never had the heart to tell her that the Confederacy had lost the War, that her slaves had become free and departed, that her disreputable overseer had acquired Blake Hall, and that she and her children were living as tenants in the old overseer's cabin. Only lies could be spoken in her presence.[2]

Those who could not so insulate themselves had to find their places somewhere in the free-labor world that had displaced their own. Most of them drifted into the most conservative sector of Unionist opinion, and became racist Democrats. A few went much farther in their transition, and became Republicans and progressives. One way or other, they became "reconstructed." As the years passed, they pruned more and more antebellum vestiges from their new worldview. "It would be great folly," one of them pointed out, "for anyone belonging to our generation to be twitting his neighbor on inconsistency in opinion in regard to public affairs during the last twenty years. . . ."[3]

Having lost their proslavery worldview, reconstructed Southerners were no longer the men they had been. A Baptist publication in Richmond, calling for Confederate resistance in the fall of 1864, had predicted that a loss of identity would be the price of Confederate defeat. The conflict was not one of interests, it pointed out, but of the principles that underlay Southern society." . . . [A] people cannot change principles," it warned, "without becoming another people—without dying to what it was, and rising again to what it was not."[4] The Confederates who survived the War underwent the conversion that the author feared.

Pollard himself marveled at the more extreme cases of conversion. "Men who were formerly esteemed good Democrats," he noticed, "assert now an extreme position in the ranks of Radicalism; men who were once incandescent secessionists . . . are willing to become the sucking doves of negrophilism and the tools of enemies whom, in their former lives they held as hereditary. . . ."[5] He himself, though, was going through the same process in a milder form. Southerners' antebellum histories were, indeed, "former lives"—previous incarnations. Having found roles in a new social order, and self-understandings in a new worldview, they had become new persons.

Pollard and some others made the change of their worldview bearable by falsifying their memories to make their past harmonious with their postbellum environment. That was what Pollard did in *The Lost Cause Regained* and in his articles on John C. Calhoun and on "The Anti-Slavery Men of the South." To reduce the cognitive dissonance between his old and new worldviews, he tried to establish continuity between the cause he had previously championed and the one he was newly adopting. In that task, he did not work for himself alone. After his conversion he addressed other former Confederates as an advocate of adaptation to Northern norms. His earlier career as an exponent of Southern nationalism gave him a claim to their attention and respect. For many of them, his persuasiveness would depend on his ability to convince them that the new cause was compatible with the old one. For their sake and his own, Pollard tried to harmonize the two causes.

He might have argued that his effort was a legitimate reinterpretation of history. After an "historical convulsion," he believed, "retrospective self-enlightenment" would reveal what had been the "mere idols" of the past and "what should have been its true aspirations." The rapid adaptation many former Confederates had made to postbellum life suggested to him that ideas suited to that life must have been latent in the Southern mind before the events of 1865 awakened them. Pollard might therefore conclude that the old order had not been as different from the new as it had appeared. From his standpoint, that would appear plausible enough.[6]

His "Lost Cause Regained" speculations also reflected, though, the working of a psychological defense mechanism appropriate to the defeated Confederates' situation. People understand themselves in terms of their histories, and overstepping the limits of their accustomed worldview makes them uncomfortable. Even revolutionary innovators, as Karl Marx pointed out, instinctively "conjure up the spirits of the past to their service and borrow from them names, battle cries and costumes in order to present the new scene of world history in this time-honored disguise and in this adopted language."[7] Slaveholders who had staked everything on the effort to save their ancestral way of life felt a much greater need to legitimate their adaptation by disguising it. The dissonance between their "Lost Cause" and their participation in the system that had supplanted it constituted a heavy mental burden.

Some resolved the dissonance by falsifying or muting their dissonant memories. Falsifying did not have to mean altering conscious recollections of events. It might mean revising recollections only at the subconscious level, or projecting a later state of mind into recollections of one's external activities. Pollard showed signs of falsifying his personal past in both of those ways. A fictional subconscious autobiography may have prompted him in 1868 to refer to the Republican rhetoric that "we" heard during the War,[8] and to sign the "iron clad oath" of wartime loyalty. He projected a later attitude into his early activities when he came to regard *Black Diamonds* as motivated by his later enlightenment about blacks. Those signs that he revised his personal past paralleled the social role that his harmonizing reinterpretations played.

For former Confederates as a group, Pollard's "Lost Cause Regained" idea and later "nationalist" reinterpretations served as a falsification of collective memory, smoothing over the transition from the Old South to the new America. As Mrs. Blake enjoyed a present falsified to adjust it to the antebellum past, other former Confederates falsified the South's past to adjust it to their postbellum world. They projected the free-labor and Unionist worldview they had adopted into the roles they had played as Confederates. The Confederacy, they came to believe, had stood only for white supremacy and constitutional limitations. As long, therefore, as white men governed by limited powers, they could reassure themselves that the essence of their "Lost Cause" still remained with them. Their children, growing up in the new system and imbibing their elders' revised memory, might never realize that their forefathers had believed in and loved the system of slavery.

One of Pollard's favorite historical personages, ironically, was Cola de Rienzi, who at the beginning of the fourteenth century had tried to revive the tribunate and other institutions of the ancient Roman Republic.[9] Rienzi was as powerless to revive ancient Rome as the "reconstructed" Pollard was to restore the Old South—but his appropriation of ancient symbols gave an aura of legitimacy to his largely innovative program. Similarly, Pollard used the idea of "the Lost Cause Regained" to legitimate the triumphant North's social and political system in the eyes of those who still measured legitimacy by the standard of "the Lost Cause" on which they had staked their lives.

NOTES

I THE TWO WORLDS OF EDWARD A. POLLARD

1. New York *Times*, February 1, 1869, p. 4.
2. The best of those sketches is James Southall Wilson, "Edward Alfred Pollard," in Edwin A. Alderman, Joel Chandler Harris, and Charles W. Kent, eds., *Library of Southern Literature, Compiled under the Direct Supervision of Southern Men of Letters* (New Orleans, Atlanta, and Dallas: Martin and Hoyt, 1907), IX, 4147-50. See also "Edward A. Pollard," in *The American Annual Cyclopedia and Register of Important Events, 1872* (New York: D. Appleton and Sons, 1872), p. 676, and James G. de Roulhac Hamilton, "Edward A. Pollard," in Allen Johnson and Dumas Malone, eds., *Dictionary of American Biography* (New York: Charles Scribner's Sons, 1928-1937), XV, 47-48.
3. Alexander Brown, *The Cabells and Their Kin: A Memorial Volume of History, Biography, and Genealogy* (Boston and New York: Houghton, Mifflin and Company, 1895), 219, 406-7, 433-34; Michael Houston, "Edward A. Pollard and the Richmond *Examiner*: A Study of Journalistic Opposition in Wartime" (M. A. thesis, American University, 1963), pp. 27-30. To Houston's reasons for dating Pollard's birth in 1832, one may add his age as given in U.S. Census Manuscripts, Schedule 1: Population, Lynch Ward, City of Lynchburg, Campbell County, Virginia, 1870, p. 56.
4. Wilson, "Pollard," p. 4147; Houston, "Pollard, pp. 34-48. Reminiscences of Pollard's plantation youth appear throughout Edward. A. Pollard, *Black Diamonds Gathered in the Darkey Homes of the South* (New York: Pudney and Russell, 1859).
5. Pollard, *Black Diamonds*, pp. 21, 43-45; *The San Francisco Directory for 1854* (San Francisco: n.p., 1854), pp. 109, 231; Edward C. Kemble, *A History of California Newspapers, 1846-1858*, edited by Helen Harding Bretnor (Los Gatos, Cal.: Talisman Press, 1962), pp. 123, 369.
6. New York *Herald*, May 24, 1856, p. 1; Edward A. Pollard, "Modern Analogies to the Roman History," *Southern Literary Messenger* (Richmond, Va.), XXIV (May, 1857), 354; Washington *Union*, May 14, 1857, p. 2, June 3, 1857, p. 2, and June 11, 1857, p. 2; Edward A. Pollard, *A New Southern Policy, or The Slave Trade as Meaning Union and Conservatism* (n.p., [1858]), p. 1.
7. On his early literary ambitions, see A. E. [sic] Pollard, "Scraps of Thought," *Southern Literary Messenger*, XVII (March, 1851), 160; Edward A. Pollard, "Stray Writings," *Southern Literary Messenger*, XVIII (August, 1852), 468-69.
8. Southall, "Pollard," p. 4148; Edward A. Pollard, "A Re-Gathering of 'Black Diamonds' in the Old Dominion," *Southern Literary Messenger*, XXIX (October, 1859), 294.
9. Edward A. Pollard to George W. Bagby, June 21, 1860; Pollard to Bagby, August 1, 1860; Pollard to Bagby, October 23, 1860; all in George W. Bagby Papers, Virginia Historical Society.
10. [Edward A. Pollard], *Letters of the Southern Spy, in Washington and Elsewhere* (Baltimore: n.p., 1861), pp. 5-12, 36, 48, [93-95]; New York *Times*, November 26, 1868, p. 1.

11. Edward A. Pollard, *Observations in the North: Eight Months in Prison and on Parole* (Richmond: E. W. Ayres, 1865), p. 16; John B. Jones, *A Rebel War Clerk's Diary at the Confederate States Capital*, edited by Howard Swiggett (New York: Old Hickory Bookshop, 1935), II, 158; Edward A. Pollard, *A Tract for Coloured People: A Letter of Advice and Exhortation to the Coloured People of Virginia* (Lynchburg, Va.: Schaffter and Bryant, 1869), p. 4; George W. Bagby, *The Old Virginia Gentleman and Other Sketches*, edited with an introduction by Thomas Nelson Page (New York: Charles Scribner's Sons, 1911), pp. 217-29; see Francis W. Dawson to Mary Perking Reeks, January 7, 1866, Dawson to Reeks, January 11, 1866, Dawson to Mr. or Mrs. Tyler, [February 16, 1866], Dawson to Louisa T. Haxall, March 3, 1866, all in Francis Warrington Dawson Papers, Duke University.

12. Houston, "Pollard," pp. 3, 63-66; Richmond *Examiner*, July 16, 1862, p. 2; scattered *Examiner* payroll records, March 1, 1862-January 21, 1865, in Daniel-Moncure Papers, University of Virginia; Edward A. Pollard to Messrs. West and Johnston, May 23, 1863, manuscript collection, University of Virginia. On Daniel's management of the *Examiner*, see George W. Bagby, "John M. Daniel's Latch-Key," in Bagby, *Old Virginia Gentleman*, pp. 166-216, and Robert W. Hughes, *"Editors of the Past": Lecture of Judge Robert W. Hughes Delivered before the Virginia Press Association at Their Annual Meeting at Charlottesville, Va., on the 22nd of June, 1897* (Richmond: Wm. Ellis Jones, 1897), pp. 17-30.

13. Pollard, *Southern Spy*, pp. [93-95]; Pollard, *Observations*, pp. 10n, 30, 34-35, 39-42, 66, 68-69.

14. *Ibid.*, pp. 9-130; New York *Times*, May 21, 1864, p. 1; R. N. Scott et al., eds., *War of the Rebellion: A Compilation of the Official Records of the Union and Confederate Armies* (Washington: Government Printing Office, 1880-1901), Series I, Volume XLII, Part III, 782; Ser. II, Vol. VII, 1035, 1160; Vol. VIII, 88-89.

15. New York *Times*, April 12, 1865, p. 1; Scott et al., eds., *Official Records*, Ser. I, Vol. XLVI, Part III, 895.

16. Edward A. Pollard to Robert E. Lee, October 4, 1865, and copy of Lee to Pollard, October 12, 1865, from Lee Letter Book (1865-1866), both items in Robert E. Lee Headquarters Papers, Virginia Historical Society; Richmond *Examiner*, July 25, 1866, p. 2. Pollard's name appeared on the *Avalanche*'s masthead from January 1 to March 23, 1866.

17. Richmond *Dispatch*, July 24, 1866, p. 2; Richmond *Examiner*, July 25, 1866, p. 2; New York *Times*, July 1, 1866, p. 3.

18. Sketch in Alderman, Harris, and Kent, eds., *Library of Southern Literature*, XV, 349; New York *Times*, June 17, 1868, p. 8, June 19, 1868, p. 3, and June 24, 1868, p. 5.

19. [Edward A. Pollard], manuscript draft of prospectus or editorial for *Southern Opinion* [May or June, 1867?], Robert Alonzo Brock Collection, Henry E. Huntington Library, San Marino, California; cf. *Southern Opinion* (Richmond), June 15, 1867, p. 2, with Edward A. Pollard, *The Lost Cause: A New Southern History of the War of the Confederates* (New York: E. B. Treat and Company, 1867), p. 751.

20. Pollard, *Lost Cause*, pp. [i-ii]; [Daniel Harvey Hill], "The Lost Dispatch," *The Land We Love* (Charlotte, N.C.), IV (February, 1868), 270-84; [Daniel Harvey Hill], editorial, *Land We Love*, VI (July, 1868), 281-85; Jubal A. Early, "Popular Errors in Regard to the Battles of the War," *Land We Love*, VI (February, 1869), 276-77; Pierre G. T. Beauregard, "Notes on E. A. Pollard's *Lost*

Cause," *The Southern Magazine* (Baltimore), X (February, 1872), 163-71; Charles Marshall to D. H. Hill, November 11, 1867, Joseph E. Johnston to Hill, June 26, 1868, and Johnston to Hill, January 29, 1869, all in Daniel Harvey Hill Papers, Virginia State Library; *Southern Opinion*, May 23, 1868, p. 1.

21. Baltimore *Sun*, November 15, 16, 19, 20, and 26, 1867; New York *Times*, November 15, 1867, p. 1.

22. Baltimore *Sun*, January 29 and 30 and February 11, 1868; New York *Times*, January 29 and 30, February 1, June, 17, 19, and 24, 1868, and June 30, 1869.

23. New York *Times*, December 6 and 9, 1868; January 29 and February 1, 1869.

24. *Southern Opinion*, December 5, 1868, pp. 1-3, and March 13, 1869, p. 2; New York *Times*, November 25, 26, 27, 30, 1868, March 1 and 7, 1869; Edward A. Pollard, *Memoir of the Assassination of Henry Rives Pollard* (Lynchburg: Schaffter and Bryant, 1869), pp. 3-32; William Porcher Miles Diary (November 27-29, 1868), William Porcher Miles Papers, University of North Carolina at Chapel Hill.

25. Pollard, *Tract for Coloured People*, pp. 2, 16; Edward A. Pollard, *The Virginia Tourist: Sketches of the Springs and Mountains of Virginia* (Philadelphia: J. B. Lippincott and Company, 1870), pp. 37-273.

26. Pollard, *Tract for Coloured People*, p. 3; U.S. Census Manuscripts, Schedule 1: Population, Lynch Ward, City of Lynchburg, Campbell County, Virginia, 1870, p. 56; Edward A. Pollard, "The Negro in the South," *Lippincott's Magazine* (New York), V (April, 1870), 383, 389; Houston, "Pollard," p. 47; Richmond *Enquirer*, December 18, 1872, p. 2.

27. Richmond *Enquirer*, December 18, 1872, p. 2.

28. See Lawrence J. Friedman, *The White Savage: Racial Fantasies in the Postbellum South* (Engelwood Cliffs, N.J.: Prentice-Hall, 1970), p. 25; Houston, "Pollard," pp. 44-45.

29. Ulrich B. Phillips, "The Central Theme of Southern History," *American Historical Review*, XXXIV (October, 1928), 30-31, 42-43. See Eugene D. Genovese's critique, "Race and Class in Southern History: An Appraisal of the Work of Ulrich Bonnell Phillips," *Agricultural History*, XLI (October, 1967), 345-58.

30. Ulrich B. Phillips, *The Course of the South to Secession: An Interpretation*, edited by E. Merton Coulter (New York and London: D. Appleton-Century Company, 1939), pp. 124-26.

31. Phillips, "Central Theme," pp. 40-41; Phillips, *Course of the South*, pp. 126-27.

32. James A. Rawley, *Race and Politics: "Bleeding Kansas" and the Coming of the Civil War* (Philadelphia and New York: J. B. Lippincott Company, 1970), pp. 261-62.

33. Thomas P. Govan devised that formulation of the question in his article, "Was the Old South Different?", in *Journal of Southern History*, XXI (November, 1955), 447-55.

34. A classic illustration of that approach is Howard W. Odum, *Southern Regions of the United States* (Chapel Hill: University of North Carolina Press, 1936).

35. Harriet Beecher Stowe, *Uncle Tom's Cabin, or Life among the Lowly* (Modern Library edition; New York: Random House, 1938), p. 229.

36. See Carl Becker, *The Declaration of Independence: A Study in the History of Political Ideas* (Vintage edition: New York: Vintage Books, 1942), pp. 243-56; Roy F. Nichols, *The Disruption of American Democracy* (New

York: Macmillan, 1948), pp. 196-97, 241-42, 333; E. Merton Coulter, *The Confederate States of America, 1861-1865* (Baton Rouge: Louisiana State University Press, 1950), pp. 62-67.

37. Their fears are well summarized in Dwight L. Dumond, *The Secession Movement, 1860-1861* (New York: Macmillan, 1931), pp. 113-20. For an extended secessionist argument that Republican administrations could undermine slavery by a series of indirect steps, without abrupt or obviously unconstitutional measures, see Edmund Ruffin's prophetic novel *Anticipations of the Future, To Serve as Lessons for the Present Time, in the Form of Extracts of Letters from an English Resident of the United States, to the London Times, from 1864 to 1870, with an Appendix, on the Causes and Consequences of the Independence of the South* (Richmond: J. W. Randolph, 1860), pp. 1-82, 103-8.

38. Montgomery *Daily Post*, December 24, 1860, in Dwight L. Dumond, ed., *Southern Editorials on Secession* (New York: Appleton-Century-Crofts, 1931), pp. 369-70.

39. See below, pp. 50-55, and Jack P. Maddex, Jr., *The Virginia Conservatives, 1867-1879: A Study in Reconstruction Politics* (Chapel Hill: University of North Carolina Press, 1970), pp. 125-30, 184-203.

40. Among recent writers, see particularly Raimondo Luraghi, "The Civil War and the Modernization of American Society: Social Structure and Industrial Revolution in the Old South before and during the War," *Civil War History*, XVIII (September, 1972), 230-50.

41. The "consensus school" of the 1950's enjoyed no monopoly on that thesis, although it did have the distinction of carrying it to its logical conclusion. Two interesting attempts to assimilate the Civil War era into the consensus pattern are Louis Hartz, "The Feudal Dream of the South," in *The Liberal Tradition in America* (New York: Harcourt Brace and World, 1955), pp. 145-200, and Daniel J. Boorstin, "The Civil War and the Democratic Process," in *The Genius of American Politics* (Chicago: University of Chicago Press, 1953), pp. 99-132.

42. W. E. B. DuBois, *Black Reconstruction in America: An Essay toward a History of the Part which Black Folk Played in the Attempt to Reconstruct Democracy in America, 1860-1880* (New York: Harcourt Brace, 1935), pp. 8-9.

43. Jonathan Wiener, "Plantations, Politics, and Industry: Alabama, 1850-1890," Ph.D. dissertation, Harvard University, 1972.

44. Paul M. Gaston, *The New South Creed: A Study in Southern Mythmaking* (New York: Alfred A. Knopf, 1970).

45. "In the South," Mark Twain observed in 1883, "the war is what A.D. is elsewhere; they date time from it. All day long you hear things 'placed' as having happened since the waw; or du'in' the waw; or right aftah the waw; or 'bout two yeahs or five yeahs or ten yeahs befo' the waw or aftah the waw." Mark Twain (Samuel L. Clemens), *Life on the Mississippi*, in *The Writings of Mark Twain* (New York and London: Harper and Brothers, 1911), IX, 336-37.

46. Eva R. Jones, in Robert Manson Myers, ed., *The Children of Pride: A True Story of Georgia and the Civil War* (New Haven and London: Yale University Press, 1972), p. 1273; George Anderson Mercer, quoted in Clement Eaton, *The Waning of the Old South Civilization, 1860-1880* (Athens, Ga.: University of Georgia Press, 1968), p. 113; J. Randolph Tucker to R. M. T. Hunter, November 9, 1869, Hunter-Garnett Papers, University of Virginia.

47. See Fitzhugh Lee, quoted in Baltimore *Sun*, July 3, 1866, p. 1; Mary Boykin Chesnut, *A Diary from Dixie*, edited by Ben Ames Williams (Cambridge, Mass.: Houghton Mifflin, 1949), pp. 544, 547; John S. Wise, *The End of an Era* (Boston and New York: Houghton Mifflin, 1899), pp. 461-63; Robert E.

Withers, *The Autobiography of an Octogenarian* (Roanoke, Va.: Stone Printing and Manufacturing Company, 1907), p. 227.
  48. See references in Maddex, *Virginia Conservatives*, pp. 123-25.
  49. C. Vann Woodward, *The Origins of the New South, 1877-1913* (Baton Rouge, La.: Louisiana State University Press, 1951), pp. 14, 154-55.
  50. Paul H. Buck, *The Road to Reunion, 1865-1900* (Boston: Little, Brown and Company, 1937), pp. 236-62; Thomas J. Pressly, *Americans Interpret Their Civil War* (Princeton, N.J.: Princeton University Press, 1954), pp. 121-92; Sheldon Van Auken, "The Southern Historical Novel in the Early Twentieth Century," *Journal of Southern History*, XIV (May, 1948), 157-91.

II THE OLD SOUTH CREED, 1832-1867

  1. Edward A. Pollard, "The Real Condition of the South," *Lippincott's Magazine*, VI (December, 1870), 612.
  2. Edward A. Pollard, "The Story of a Hero," *The Galaxy* (New York), VI (November, 1868), 599; *Southern Opinion*, December 5, 1868, p. 3; Pollard, *Black Diamonds*, p. 97.
  3. Records from 1845, 1850, and 1860 show the number of slaves on the Oakridge estate ranging from 104 to 120. Austin Embrey (Clerk, Circuit Court of Nelson County, Virginia) to the author, April 20, 1972, in author's possession; U.S. Census Manuscripts, Schedule 2; Slave Population, Nelson County, Virginia, 1850, columns 959-60, 962-63; 1860, pp. 16-17, 24-25.
  4. (Leavenworth) *Weekly Kansas Herald*, April 13, 1855, p. 2.
  5. Pollard, *Black Diamonds*, pp. 21-22, 43-44; Edward A. Pollard, "The Story of a California Faro-Table," *Southern Literary Messenger*, XXXII (January, 1861), 37-44.
  6. *San Francisco Directory, 1854*, p. 109; editor's note in Kemble, *California Newspapers*, p. 369; *Weekly Kansas Herald*, August 4, 1855, p. 2, and September 1, 1855, p. 2; New York *Herald*, May 24, 1856, p. 1; New York *Tribune*, May 24, 1856, p. 7; Washington *Union*, May 14, 1857, p. 2, June 3, 1857, p. 2, and June 11, 1857, p. 2; Pollard, *Black Diamonds*, pp. 111-13. Identification of Pollard as the correspondent "Exile" is not certain but highly probable. Pollard claimed personal information indicating that slavery expansion had been one of Walker's motives in going to Nicaragua. Pollard, *Black Diamonds*, p. 111.
  7. William Walker, *The War in Nicaragua* (Mobile, Ala.: S. H. Goetzel, 1860), p. 265; Edward A. Pollard, *New Southern Policy*, p. 1; Washington *Union*, June 11, 1857, p. 2; Pollard, *Black Diamonds*, pp. 111-12, 114.
  8. Pollard, *Black Diamonds*, pp. 21-22, 25, 27-28, 30-34, 48-51, 58-60, 72-81, 88-89, 92-95, 98-99, 118-19.
  9. *Ibid.*, pp. 30, 38-45, 80-81, 84-85, 88-98, 115-22. For other expressions of Pollard's preoccupation with loved ones' deaths, see [Edward A. Pollard], "The Mourner's Portfolio," *Southern Literary Messenger*, XXXI (November, 1860), 351-58, and [Edward A. Pollard], "More Leaves from a Mourner's Portfolio," *Southern Literary Messenger*, XXXI (December, 1860), 441-43.
  10. Pollard, *Black Diamonds*, pp. 21, 31-33, 38, 41, 43-47, 51, 85-87, 95; Edward A. Pollard, *The Third Year of the War* (New York: C. B. Richardson, 1865), p. 196.
  11. Pollard, *Black Diamonds*, pp. 20, 22, 50-51, 81-88, 117; [Edward A. Pollard], *Black Aaron: A Christmas Story for His Little Nephews* (New York: Pudney and Russell, 1859), pp. 5-17.
  12. Pollard, *Black Diamonds*, pp. 25-29; Pollard, *Black Aaron*, pp. 6-9, 14-15.

13. Pollard, *Black Diamonds*, pp. 106-7.
14. *Ibid.*, pp. 19-20, 37, 55-59, 61-62; Pollard, *New Southern Policy*, pp. 1-2; Edward A. Pollard to Horace Greeley, April [n.d.], 1860, in Edward A. Pollard, "The Anti-Slavery Men of the South," *Galaxy*, XVI (September, 1873), 337-38; Edward A. Pollard, "The Romance of the Negro," *Galaxy*, XII (October, 1871), 472.
15. Pollard, *Black Diamonds*, pp. 52-55, 63-69, 107-15; Pollard, *New Southern Policy*, pp. 1-8.
16. Ronald T. Takaki, *A Pro-Slavery Crusade: The Agitation to Reopen the African Slave Trade* (New York: Free Press, 1971), pp. 27-32; Edward A. Pollard, "Hints on Southern Civilization," *Southern Literary Messenger*, XXXII (March, 1861), pp. 308-11.
17. Edward A. Pollard to George W. Bagby, August 1, 1860, and Pollard to Bagby, October 23, 1860, both in Bagby Family Papers; Pollard, "Hints on Southern Civilization," p. 311; [Pollard], *Southern Spy*, pp. 3, 8, 27; New York *Times*, June 19, 1868, p. 3.
18. [Pollard], *Southern Spy*, pp. 6-8, 13-21, 27-80, [93-95]; Pollard, "Story of a Hero," pp. 599-600.
19. *Ibid.*, pp. 17-18; Richmond *Examiner*, June 26 and 27, July 4, 14, 24, and 29, August 4, 9, and 16, 1862; Edward A. Pollard, *The First Year of the War* (Richmond: West and Johnston, 1862), pp. 12-40, 57-58, 264, 357; Edward A. Pollard, *The Second Year of the War* (New York: Charles B. Richardson, 1864), pp. 178, 227-29, 294-302, 305. Because of the difficulty of determining authorship of particular editorials, I have cited the *Examiner* only for the months when Pollard exercised editorial control of the paper. During that time he presumably rewrote the editorials he did not personally compose, as Daniel did at other times. Richmond *Examiner*, July 16, 1862, p. 2.
20. Pollard, *First Year*, pp. 339-40, 357; Richmond *Examiner*, June 30, July 1, 3, 5, 17, 18, 19, 21, 22, 23, 25, 26, 29, 30, 31, August 2, 4, 5, 7, 8, 13, 15, 16, 20, 25, 29, 30, 1862; Pollard, *Third Year*, pp. 197-207; Pollard, *Observations*, pp. 33-38, 49-51, 60, 87-88, 112.
21. Richmond *Examiner*, August 18, 19, 21, and 28, 1862; Pollard, *Observations*, pp. 133-35.
22. Richmond *Examiner*, July 29 and 30, August 1, 2, 7, 22, and 23, 1862; Pollard, *Observations*, pp. 93-97, 101-3, 127; Pollard, *First Year*, pp. 263-64, 344-46, 357-59; Pollard, *Second Year*, p. 182; Pollard, *Third Year*, pp. 187-96.
23. Richmond *Examiner*, June 28, July 7, 14, 15, 24, and 25, 1862; Pollard, *First Year*, pp. 355-57, 359-60; Pollard, *Second Year*, pp. 289-90; Pollard, *Observations*, pp. 128-29.
24. Pollard, *Observations*, pp. 29-30, 71-72, 80-85, 126-36; Edward A. Pollard, *A Letter to the State of the War, by One Recently Returned from the Enemy's Country* (Richmond: n.p., [1865]), pp. 1-8.
25. New York *Times*, April 12, 1865, p. 1; Scott *et al.*, eds., *Official Records*, Ser. I, Vol. XLVI, Part III, 895; Philadelphia *Inquirer*, April 19, 1865, p. 1, and April 21, 1865, p. 4.
26. See Edward A. Pollard to Robert E. Lee, October 4, 1865, Lee Headquarters Papers.
27. Edward A. Pollard, *Southern History of the War* (two-volume edition; New York: Charles B. Richardson, 1865), II, 501-2, 581-608; cf. two-volume-in-one edition, 1866.
28. Pollard, *Lost Cause*, pp. 742-49.

29. *Ibid.*, pp. 749-52.
30. Even the most loyal Southern nationalists, after 1865, suffered from those doubts. The *Southern Opinion* conceded in an early issue that "the South, considered as a great nationality, as a people of peculiar habits and instinct, . . . is now but an empire of the past." It was "[o]f the South, however, as she *was*, not as she *may* be," that the paper was mainly intended to speak. *Southern Opinion*, June 23, 1867, p. 2.
31. Text from C. C. Davis, "Elegant Old Rebel," *Virginia Cavalcade*, VIII (summer, 1958), 42-43. Punctuation supplied.
32. Pollard, *Lost Cause*, pp. 645-46, 652-53, 657, 659, 727, 729.
33. *Ibid.*, "Introduction to the New and Enlarged Edition," pp. [i-ii]; pp. 90-91, 414, 554, 681-84, 763-76; Edward A. Pollard, *Life of Jefferson Davis, with a Secret History of the Southern Confederacy, Gathered "behind the Scenes" at Richmond* (Philadelphia: National Publishing Company, 1869), p. iv; Edward A. Pollard, "The Last Council-Board of the Southern Confederacy," *Southern Home Journal* (Baltimore), November 23, 1867, p. 4; Edward A. Pollard, "Jefferson Davis as an Orator," *Southern Home Journal*, December 7, 1867, pp. 4-5. Pollard also neglected some obvious points on which to criticize Davis. See Pollard, *Lost Cause*, pp. 246-50, 381, 415-28.
34. Edward A. Pollard, *Lee and His Lieutenants: Comprising the Early Life, Public Services, and Campaigns of General Robert E. Lee and His Companions in Arms, with a Record of Their Campaigns and Heroic Deeds* (New York: E. B. Treat, 1867), pp. 848-51.
35. *Ibid.* Pollard was not alone in his expectations. Other unreconstructed Southern nationalists continued for years after 1865 to hope for the achievement of Southern independence. They included Confederate States Senator Louis Wigfall, Fr. Abram J. Ryan, and Robert Barnwell Rhett, Jr. Alvy L. King, *Louis T. Wigfall: Southern Fire-Eater* (Baton Rouge: Louisiana State University Press, 1970), pp. 228-229; *Southern Opinion*, October 3, 1868, p. 2, and March 13, 1869, p. 1.
36. Pollard, *Lost Cause*, pp. 753-59. This appendix to the 1867 edition shows that the idea of alliance with Northern racists was beginning to appeal to Pollard.
37. Pollard, *Lost Cause*, pp. 46-50; Pollard, *Third Year*, pp. 293-94; Pollard, *Southern History*, II, 566.
38. Pollard, *Lost Cause*, pp. 48-51, 359-60; Pollard, *Southern History*, II, 566-69. Pollard's belief that slavery had given the Southern gentry its character led him to argue in 1858 that acquiring slaves would ennoble a degraded "poor white" and "transform him into another man." Pollard, *Black Diamonds*, p. 54.
39. Pollard, *Lost Cause*, pp. 49-52; Pollard, "Hints on Southern Civilization," pp. 308-11; Pollard, *Second Year*, pp. 292-305; Pollard, *Third Year*, pp. 294-98; Pollard, *Southern History*, II, 532; Richmond *Examiner*, July 2, 12, and 14, August 4 and 26, 1862; Pollard, *Observations*, pp. 128-29.
40. Pollard, *Lost Cause*, pp. 33-34, 37-39, 45, 51-52, 58; Pollard, *Southern History*, II, 530-43, 579-80.
41. Pollard, *Lost Cause*, pp. 51, 101, 115, 129-31, 175-78, 181, 185-86, 561-63, 682; Pollard, *Second Year*, pp. 300-5; Pollard, *Third Year*, pp. 298-302; Pollard, *Observations*, pp. 92-97.
42. Pollard, *Lost Cause*, pp. 62, 68-70, 80, 113-15, 299, 357-58, 361-62, 465-70, 508, 557, 561-75; Pollard, *Observations*, pp. 30-31, 48, 61, 72-78, 88. 90.
43. *Southern Opinion*, August 24, 1867, p. 2. The paper used the archaic *-ck* word endings.

III A DISGUISED SURRENDER, 1867-1868

1. See Edward A. Pollard, "The Living Politicians of To-Day: Salmon P. Chase," *Southern Home Journal*, March 28, 1868, p. 5.
2. Charles H. Coleman, *The Election of 1868: The Democratic Effort to Regain Control* (New York: Columbia University Press, 1933), pp. 48-54; Maddex, *Virginia Conservatives*, pp. 54-55; *Southern Opinion*, September 14, 1867, p. 2; Edward A. Pollard, *The Lost Cause Regained* (New York: G. W. Carleton and Company, 1868), pp. 142-43, 163n. The *Southern Opinion* writer "Pilgrim," who first appeared as a reverent visitor to battlefields, shifted his attention to conservative politics by a course particularly similar to Pollard's. "Pilgrim" apparently was J. Marshall Hanna of Richmond. *Southern Opinion*, October 5, November 9 and 23, 1867.
3. Prospectus in *Southern Opinion*, November 23, 1867, p. 3.
4. Edward A. Pollard, "The Growth and Greatness of America," excerpts reprinted from New York *News* (issue unidentified) in *Southern Opinion*, December 28, 1867, p. 2. The "Living Politicians of To-Day" series ran in the *Southern Home Journal* from February 22 to May 23, 1868, except for the April 4 and May 9 issues.
5. Edward A. Pollard, "Personal Recollections of John C. Calhoun," New York *Citizen*, May 9, 1868, p. 2. Compare the attitude to secession in Edward A. Pollard, "The Living Politicians of To-Day: Andrew Johnson," *Southern Home Journal*, February 22, 1868, pp. 4-5.
6. Pollard, *Lost Cause Regained*, pp. 13-14, 110-11, 155, 214.
7. *Southern Opinion*, July 11, 1868, p. 3; *The Political Pamphlet* (New York), September 12, 1868, p. 26; New York *Times*, August 31, 1868, p. 2.
8. Pro-Southern critics applauded the book's political sections but criticized the strictures on Davis in Chapter I. Republicans enjoyed Chapter I, but disliked the remainder. *Southern Home Journal*, July 25, 1868, p. 4; *The Old Guard* (New York), VI (September, 1868), 715-16; New York *Times*, August 31, 1868, p. 2.
9. Pollard, *Lost Cause Regained*, p. 16.
10. *Ibid.*, pp. 19-36, 40-44.
11. *Ibid.*, pp. 21-23, 25-29, 31-32, 39-41, 44-45, 48.
12. *Ibid.*, pp. 20-21, 34, 55. The only comparable suggestion in Pollard's previous writings was Pollard, *Lost Cause*, pp. 488-89.
13. Pollard, *Lost Cause Regained*, pp. 58-68, 169-70, 173-76.
14. *Ibid.*, pp. 63-66, 86-94.
15. *Ibid.*, 132-39.
16. *Ibid.*, pp. 15, 59-60, 68-69, 84-85, 105-8, 132, 168.
17. *Ibid.*, pp. 100-1, 107, 129-32, 167.
18. *Ibid.*, pp. 102, 106-7, 154.
19. *Ibid.*, pp. 13, 112-13, 115, 117-18, 154-55.
20. *Ibid.*, pp. 13, 113, 115-18, 132, 154; Pollard, *Third Year*, p. 293; Pollard, *Southern History*, II, 549. Cf. Pollard, *Lost Cause Regained*, pp. 118-28, with John H. Van Evrie, *Negroes and Negro "Slavery": The First an Inferior Race; The Latter Its Normal Condition* (New York: Van Evrie, Horton and Company, 1861). See Van Evrie's exchange with "Warwick" [William F. Samford] in New York *Day-Book*, October 19, 1867, p. 4, and December 7, 1867, pp. 4-5.
21. Pollard, *Lost Cause Regained*, pp. 14, 130, 185.
22. For a statement of that opinion in 1876, see Robert L. Dabney, *Discussions by Robert L. Dabney, D. D., LL. D., Recently Professor of Moral Philoso-

phy in the University of Texas, and for Many Years Professor of Theology in Union Theological Seminary in Virginia, edited by Clement Read Vaughan (Mexico, Mo.: Crescent Publishing House, 1897), IV, 182-84, 188.

23. Pollard, *Lost Cause Regained,* pp. 38-39, 72-73, 80-81, 128, 134-36, 138-40; New York *Day-Book,* July 8, 1868, p. 4.

24. Pollard, *Lost Cause Regained,* pp. 107-10.

25. *Ibid.,* pp. 88-89, 95-97.

26. *Ibid.,* pp. 200-6, 208, 213; cf. Pollard, *Lost Cause,* pp. 745, 747-48, 750.

27. Pollard, *Lost Cause Regained,* pp. 82-85, 160-61, 170-72, 177-84, 211.

28. *Ibid.,* pp. 19-20, 154, 210, 212.

29. Forrest G. Wood, *Black Scare: The Racist Response to Emancipation and Reconstruction* (Berkeley and Los Angeles: University of California Press, 1968), pp. 80-155; *Congressional Globe,* 40 Congress, 3 Session (1869), 672; Thomas M. Cooley, *A Treatise on the Constitutional Limitations which Rest upon the Legislative Power of the States of the American Union* (first edition; Boston: Little, Brown and Company, 1868), pp. iv, 3, 9-10, 34-35, 39-44, 69, 73-74, 87, 114-16, 173, 189, 299, 362-63.

30. Pollard, *Lost Cause Regained,* pp. 102-5, 207; cf. *ibid.,* p. 102, with Pollard, *Observations,* p. 32. See also *Political Pamphlet,* September 26, 1868, pp. 83-84.

31. Pollard, *Lost Cause Regained,* pp. 102, 107, 110-11.

32. "Hampden" [Wade Hampton III] to Andrew Johnson, [August 25, 1866], in Charles E. Cauthen, ed., *Family Letters of the Three Wade Hamptons, 1782-1901* (Columbia, S. C.: University of South Carolina Press, 1953), pp. 123-41; Charleston *Mercury,* June 27, 1868, p. 2; William Y. Thompson, *Robert Toombs of Georgia* (Baton Rouge, La.: Louisiana State University Press, 1966), pp. 221-24; "Warwick" [William F. Samford] in New York *Day-Book,* August 29, 1868, p. 5; C. W. Hugh in *Southern Presbyterian* (Columbia, S.C.), March 19, 1868, p. 1; James Barbour to James L. Kemper, June 24, 1868, Thomas S. Bocock to Kemper, June 25, 1868, and memoranda in Kemper Attorney's Journal for June 22, 25, and 29, 1868, in James Lawson Kemper Papers, University of Virginia. Cf. Dabney, *Discussions,* IV, 214.

33. The book, according to Rives Pollard's paper, was addressed mainly to Southern readers. *Southern Opinion,* July 11, 1868, p. 3.

34. Pollard, *Lost Cause Regained,* pp. 138, 140-49, 152-53.

35. *Ibid.,* pp. [5], 153, 156-62, 173-177, 212-14.

36. *Ibid.,* pp. 133-34, 163-67, 169, 188-90, 207, 211-12.

37. *Ibid.,* pp. 102, 111, 154-56.

38. *Ibid.,* pp. 163, 167-69, 207, 211-12.

39. *Ibid.,* pp. 102-5, 185-90. For the original context of the Hammond quotation, see *Cong. Globe,* 35 Cong., 1 Sess. (1858), 962.

40. Pollard, *Lost Cause Regained,* pp. 190-200, 208-10.

41. *Ibid.,* pp. 69, 162, 164, 199-210, 212-13.

42. [John H. Van Evrie], "The Lost Cause," *Old Guard,* IV (October, 1866), 630-34; New York *Day-Book,* October 19, 1867, p. 4, and August 8, 1868, p. 4.

43. Pollard, *Lost Cause Regained,* pp. 51, 108. Hughes, almost immediately after the War, had made himself conspicuous as an advocate of reunion on the victors' terms. In 1869, he joined the Republican party. *Papers Showing the Political Course of R. W. Hughes, the Republican Candidate for Governor, before and since the Fall of the Southern Confederacy in 1865; prefixed by a Biographical Sketch* (Richmond: B. W. Gillis, 1873), pp. 15-25.

44. Pollard, *Lost Cause Regained,* p. 20.

[94]   Notes, Pages 62-69

IV THE RECONSTRUCTED REBEL, 1868-1872

1. For that purpose, it had mixed effects. Southern Democrats did find the "Lost Cause Regained" appeal useful to involve alienated former Confederates in the Democratic campaign. Zebulon B. Vance, for example, tried to make his North Carolina audiences believe that "what the Confederacy fought for would be won by Seymour and Blair." Vance and others exerted a moderating influence in the South by identifying the Democratic ticket with "the Lost Cause" —but in the North, Republicans publicized their statements to identify the Democrats with slavery and rebellion. Coleman, *Election of 1868*, pp. 310-13.

2. *Political Pamphlet*, September 12, 1868, pp. 26, 30-32, 52; September 19, 1868, pp. 53-56, 59-62, 72; September 26, 1868, pp. 82, 85-87, 98.

3. *Ibid.*, September 12, 1868, pp. 35-36; September 19, 1868, pp. 64-71; September 26, 1868, pp. 77, 91-93.

4. New York *Times*, January 29, 1869, p. 2.

5. *Southern Opinion*, December 5, 1868, pp. 1-3; New York *Times*, November 25, 26, 27, 30, 1868, and March 1 and 7, 1869; Pollard, *Tract for Coloured People*, p. 10; Pollard, *Davis*, p. 152; Richard Pollard to William Mahone, August 6, 1877, William Mahone Papers, Duke University.

6. *Southern Opinion*, May 23, 1868, p. 1.

7. Pollard, *Davis*, pp. iv-v; *Southern Opinion*, October 31, 1868, p. 4; New York *Times*, August 31, 1868, p. 2.

8. Pollard, *Davis*, pp. 103-4, 452-55, 482-83.

9. *Ibid.*, pp. 104, 341-45, 405, 407-10; on the treason accusation, see below, pp. 66-67.

10. *Ibid.*, pp. v-viii, 101-2, 167, 246-47, 325-26, 330-31, 355-56, 447, 481, 528-29.

11. *Ibid.*, pp. 121, 160-63, 202-3, 220-21, 230-32, 268-97, 308-15, 417-19, 438-39, 443-44, 456-57, 470. The only general Pollard still praised unreservedly was Joseph E. Johnston—and that because of his caution, a quality Pollard had not esteemed during the War. *Ibid.*, pp. 296-97.

12. *Ibid.*, pp. 325-27, 330-31, 349-56, 473-82, 516.

13. *Ibid.*, pp. 71, 96-97, 100, 107, 261-64; see p. 528.

14. *Ibid.*, pp. 136, 162-63, 166, 193, 227, 261-64, 282, 286-87, 386-87, 475-76.

15. *Ibid.*, pp. 43-46, 52, 54, 57-68, 75-81, 89-95.

16. *Ibid.*, pp. 43-44, 49, 53-55, 68-86, 97-98, 112, 120-24, 423-31, 450-51, 482-83.

17. *Ibid.*, pp. 109-13.

18. *Ibid.*, pp. 43-46, 61-64, 82, 89-90, 93-95, 104, 112, 198-99.

19. *Ibid.*, pp. 56-63, 84-85, 88-92, 95.

20. *Ibid.*, p. 113n; cf. pp. 52-53, 95.

21. *Ibid.*, pp. iii, vii, 162-63, 198-201, 210-19, 308-9, 321, 324, 326, 332, 336. Contrast *ibid.*, pp. 422-23, with Pollard, *Lost Cause Regained*, pp. 82-84.

22. Pollard, *Davis*, pp. 282, 287, 452-55.

23. Pollard, *Davis*, pp. 272-73; Pollard, *Virginia Tourist*, p. 195.

24. See *Southern Opinion*, January 4, 1868, p. 1, and Edward A. Pollard, "Stonewall Jackson—An Historical Study," *Putnam's Magazine* (New York), II (December, 1868), 733-40.

25. Pollard, "Story of a Hero," pp. 598-605; Pollard, *Lost Cause*, p. 254; *Political Pamphlet*, September 19, 1868, pp. 63-64; Edward A. Pollard, "History of the Fourth of July," *Lippincott's Magazine*, X (July, 1872), 66; Edward A. Pollard, "The Political Literature of America," *Old and New* (New York), II (August, 1870), 167-70.

26. Edward A. Pollard, *The Key to the Ku-Klux* (Lynchburg, Va.: n.p., 1872), pp. 8-12; Pollard, "Fourth of July," pp. 58-59.
27. Pollard, *Key to the Ku-Klux*, pp. 27-28; Pollard, "Real Condition." pp. 613-15, 617-19; Pollard, "Negro in the South," pp. 386-87; Edward A. Pollard, *A Southern Historian's Appeal for Horace Greeley* (Lynchburg, Va.: Daily Republican Book and Job Printing Establishment, 1872), pp. 4-6, 9, 25-26, 33-34.
28. Pollard, "Real Condition," pp. 619-20; Pollard, "Negro in the South," p. 388; Pollard, *Key to the Ku-Klux*, p. 2; Edward A. Pollard, "Recollections of Appomattox Court-House," *Old and New*, IV (August, 1871), 172-73; Pollard, *Appeal for Greeley*, pp. 3-5; see *Political Pamphlet*, September 12, 1868, pp. 52, 56.
29. Pollard, *Appeal for Greeley*, pp. 3-12, 16, 18-27, 31-36.
30. Pollard, "Real Condition," pp. 612-13, 617, 619-20; Pollard, *Key to the Ku-Klux*, pp. 2-4, 24; Pollard, *Appeal for Greeley*, pp. 12-13.
31. Pollard, "Real Condition," p. 617; Pollard, *Appeal for Greeley*, p. 31; Edward A. Pollard, "An Apology for Wealth," *The New Eclectic Magazine* (Baltimore), VI (June, 1870), 704; Edward A. Pollard, "New Virginia," *Old and New*, V (March, 1872), 279-84, 287-88; Pollard, *Virginia Tourist*, pp. 4, 26-33, 41-47, 64-65, 92-97, 99-100, 156, 159n, 189-90, 193, 200n, 260-64, 276-77. Unreconstructed Southern traditionalists regarded Northern tourists with hostility. See *Southern Opinion*, June 15, 1867, p. 1.
32. Pollard, "Negro in the South," p. 385; Pollard, "New Virginia," pp. 283-90; Pollard, *Virginia Tourist*, pp. 264-66.
33. Pollard, *Black Diamonds*, pp. 39-51; Pollard, "Apology for Wealth," pp. 698-705.
34. Pollard, *Virginia Tourist*, pp. 18-23, 37-38, 167, 172, 202-21, 275; Pollard, "New Virginia," pp. 279-82; contrast Pollard, *Southern History*, II, 547n-548n.
35. Paul Hamilton Hayne to "My Little (H)angel," February 10, 1862, Paul Hamilton Hayne Papers, Duke University; Edward A. Pollard, "The Political Literature of America: Webster and Jefferson," *Old Guard*, VI (March, 1868), 204-15; *Political Pamphlet*, September 12, 1868, pp. 33-37, and September 26, 1868, pp. 87-88; Pollard, "Political Literature of America" (1870), pp. 165-73. On the slavery conflict's effect on literary style, see Edmund Wilson, *Patriotic Gore: Studies in the Literature of the American Civil War* (New York: Oxford University Press, 1962), pp. 635-54.
36. *Political Pamphlet*, September 12, 1868, p. 46; Pollard, "Negro in the South," pp. 383-88, 390; Pollard, "Romance of the Negro," pp. 470-78; Pollard, "Real Condition," p. 618; Pollard, "Anti-Slavery Men," pp. 339-40; "Our Monthly Gossip," *Lippincott's Magazine*, V (March, 1870), 343; Richard B. Elder [George W. Bagby], "Country Life in Virginia Now-a-Days," *Lippincott's Magazine*, IX (March, 1872), 347.
37. Pollard, *Tract for Coloured People*, pp. 10, 14-16; Pollard, "Romance of the Negro," p. 474; Pollard, "Real Condition," pp. 616-17; Pollard, *Key to the Ku-Klux*, pp. 27-32; Pollard, *Appeal for Greeley*, pp. 27-30.
38. Pollard, *Tract for Coloured People*, pp. 10-11; Pollard, *Davis*, p. 469; Pollard, "Negro in the South," pp. 384-86, 388-90; Pollard, "Real Condition," pp. 616-17; Pollard, "Romance of the Negro," p. 470; Pollard, "New Virginia," p. 287; Pollard, *Key to the Ku-Klux*, pp. 12-26, 31.
39. Pollard, *Tract for Coloured People*, pp. 2, 8-9, 11-16; Pollard, "Negro in the South," pp. 384, 386-91; Pollard, *Appeal for Greeley*, pp. 4-6; Pollard, *Key to the Ku-Klux*, pp. 30-31; Pollard, "Anti-Slavery Men," p. 341.

40. Pollard, *Virginia Tourist*, pp. 101-2, 165-75, 211-15; Edward A. Pollard, "Historic Doubts concerning Patrick Henry," *Galaxy*, X (September, 1870), 327-34; Pollard, "Fourth of July," pp. 64-66; Pollard, "Political Literature of America" (1870), pp. 170-71; Pollard, *Tract for Coloured People*, pp. 4-7; Pollard, "Real Condition," p. 615; Pollard, "Anti-Slavery Men," p. 334; Pollard, *Appeal for Greeley*, pp. 12, 14-17, 19-20; Pollard, *Key to the Ku-Klux*, pp. 6-7, 11, 16-17.

41. Pollard, "Romance of the Negro," p. 470; Pollard, *Key to the Ku-Klux*, pp. 1-2.

42. Pollard, "Romance of the Negro," p. 471; Pollard, *Key to the Ku-Klux*, p. 7.

43. Pollard, "Anti-Slavery Men," pp. 329-41; Pollard, *Tract for Coloured People*, p. 6; Pollard, "Romance of the Negro," pp. 472-73; Pollard, *Key to the Ku-Klux*, p. 11.

44. Pollard, "Anti-Slavery Men," pp. 339, 341.

45. *Annual Cyclopedia*, 1872, p. 676.

46. Richmond *Enquirer*, December 18, 1872, p. 3; Alexander Rives to William Cabell Rives, November 12, 1867, William Cabell Rives Papers, Library of Congress; *Southern Opinion*, October 5 and November 2, 1867, and December 5, 1868; William Porcher Miles Diary (December 17-18, 1872), Miles Papers; personal inspection of Oakridge cemetery, August, 1971.

V CONCLUSIONS AND IMPLICATIONS

1. C. Vann Woodward, *The Strange Career of Jim Crow* (New York: Oxford University Press, 1955), p. 3.

2. Ellen Glasgow, *The Deliverance: A Romance of the Virginia Tobacco Fields* (New York: Doubleday, Page and Company, 1904), pp. 67-74. Mrs. Blake's story was that of an actual Southern woman in the aftermath of the War. Ellen Glasgow, *A Certain Measure: An Interpretation of Prose Fiction* (New York: Harcourt, Brace and Company, 1938), pp. 26, 35-36, 45.

3. William Henry Ruffner, in Richmond *Enquirer*, April 6, 1875, p. 1.

4. *Religious Herald* (Richmond), date unknown, reprinted in *Southern Presbyterian*, October 20, 1864, p. 2.

5. *Political Pamphlet*, September 12, 1868, p. 42.

6. Pollard, *Southern History*, II, 529-30; Pollard, "Fourth of July," p. 63; Pollard, *Davis*, p. 455.

7. Karl Marx, "The Eighteenth Brumaire of Louis Bonaparte," in Karl Marx and Frederick Engels, *Selected Works* (Moscow: Foreign Languages Publishing House, 1962), I, 247.

8. *Political Pamphlet*, September 19, 1868, p. 53.

9. Pollard, *Black Diamonds*, pp. 84-85; [Pollard], *Southern Spy*, p. 21; Pollard, "Last Council-Board," p. 4; Pollard, *Davis*, pp. 501-4.

BIBLIOGRAPHY

I POLLARD'S WRITINGS

(A) Books

Pollard, Edward A. *Black Diamonds Gathered in the Darkey Homes of the South.* New York: Pudney and Russell, 1859.

———, ed. *Echoes from the South: Comprising the Most Important Speeches, Proclamations, and Public Acts Emanating from the South during the Late War.* New York: E. B. Treat and Company, and Baltimore: L. T. Palmer and Company, [1866].

———. *The First Year of the War.* Richmond: West and Johnston, 1862.

———. *Lee and His Lieutenants: Comprising the Early Life, Public Services, and Campaigns of General Robert E. Lee and His Companions in Arms, with a Record of Their Campaigns and Heroic Deeds.* New York: E. B. Treat, 1867.

[———]. *Letters of the Southern Spy, in Washington and Elsewhere.* Baltimore: n.p., 1861.

———. *Life of Jefferson Davis, with a Secret History of the Southern Confederacy, Gathered "behind the Scenes" at Richmond.* Philadelphia: National Publishing Company, 1869.

———. *The Lost Cause: A New Southern History of the War of the Confederates.* New York: E. B. Treat, 1866. (1867 edition contains additional material significant for the present study.)

———. *The Lost Cause Regained.* New York: G. W. Carleton and Company, 1868.

———. *Observations in the North: Eight Months in Prison and on Parole.* Richmond: E. W. Ayres, 1865.

———. *The Second Year of the War.* New York: Charles B. Richardson, 1864.

———. *Southern History of the War.* 2 volumes. New York: Charles B. Richardson, 1865.

———. *The Third Year of the War.* New York: C. B. Richardson, 1865.

———. *The Virginia Tourist: Sketches of the Springs and Mountains of Virginia.* Philadelphia: J. B. Lippincott and Company, 1870.

[98] *Bibliography*

(B) Pamphlets

[Pollard, Edward A.]. *Black Aaron: A Christmas Story for His Little Nephews.* New York: Pudney and Russell, 1859.

———. *The Key to the Ku-Klux.* Lynchburg: n.p., 1872.

———. *A Letter on the State of the War, by One Recently Returned from the Enemy's Country.* Richmond: n.p., [1865].

———. *Memoir of the Assassination of Henry Rives Pollard.* Lynchburg: Schaffter and Bryant, 1869.

———. *A New Southern Policy, or the Slave Trade as Meaning Union and Conservatism.* n.p., [1858].

———. *The Rival Administrations: Richmond and Washington in December, 1863.* Richmond: for the author, 1864.

———. *The Second Battle of Manassas: with Sketches of the Recent Campaign in Northern Virginia and on the Upper Potomac.* Richmond: West and Johnston, 1862.

———. *A Southern Historian's Appeal for Horace Greeley.* Lynchburg: Daily *Republican* Book and Job Printing Establishment, 1872.

———. *A Tract for Coloured People: A Letter of Advice and Exhortation to the Coloured People of Virginia.* Lynchburg: Schaffter and Bryant, 1869.

———. *The Two Nations: A Key to the History of the American War.* Richmond: Ayres and Wade, 1864.

(C) Articles

Pollard, Edward A. "The Anti-Slavery Men of the South," *The Galaxy,* XVI (September, 1873), 329-341.

———. "An Apology for Wealth," *The New Eclectic Magazine,* VI, (June, 1870), 698-705.

———. "The Confederate Congress: A Chapter in the History of the War," *The Galaxy,* VI (December, 1869), 749-758.

———. "Hints on Southern Civilization," *Southern Literary Messenger,* XXXII (March, 1861), 308-311.

———. "History of the Fourth of July," *Lippincott's Magazine,* X (July, 1872), 56-66.

———. "Jefferson Davis as an Orator," *Southern Home Journal,* December 7, 1867, pp. 4-5.

———. "The Last Council-Board of the Southern Confederacy," *Southern Home Journal,* November 23, 1867, p. 4.

———. "The Living Politicians of To-day," series in *Southern Home Journal:* "Andrew Johnson, President of the United States," February 22, 1868, pp. 4-5; "Benjamin F. Butler," February 29, 1868, pp. 4-5; "Ulysses S. Grant," March 7, 1868, pp.

Bibliography [99]

4-5; "William H. Seward." March 14, 1868, p. 5; "Thaddeus Stevens," March 21, 1868, pp. 4-5; "Salmon P. Chase," March 28, 1868, p. 5; "Charles H. Sumner," April 11, 1868, p. 5; "Benjamin F. Wade," April 18, 1868, p. 5; "George H. Pendleton," April 25, 1868, p. 5; "Edwin M. Stanton," May 2, 1868, pp. 4-5; "Schuyler Colfax," May 16, 1868, p. 5; "Henry Wilson," May 23, 1868, p. 5.

──────. "Modern Analogies to the Roman History," *Southern Literary Messenger*, XXIV (May, 1857), 354-361.

[──────]. "More Leaves from a Mourner's Portfolio," *Southern Literary Messenger*, XXXI (December, 1860), 441-43.

[──────]. "The Mourner's Portfolio," *Southern Literary Messenger*, XXXI (November, 1860), 351-58.

──────. "The Negro in the South," *Lippincott's Magazine*, V (April, 1870), 383-91.

──────. "New Virginia," *Old and New*, V (March, 1872), 279-90.

──────. "Personal Recollections of John C. Calhoun," *New York Citizen*, May 9, 1869, p. 2.

──────. "The Political Literature of America," *Old and New*, II (August, 1870), 165-173.

──────. "The Political Literature of America: Webster and Jefferson," *The Old Guard*, VI (March, 1868), 204-215.

[──────]. "Political Science in America," *The Old Guard*, VI (July, 1868), 533-537.

──────. "The Real Condition of the South," *Lippincott's Magazine*, VI (December, 1870), 612-620.

──────. "Recollections of Appomattox Court-House," *Old and New*, IV (August, 1871), 166-175.

──────. "A Re-Gathering of 'Black Diamonds' in the Old Dominion," *Southern Literary Messenger*, XXIX (October, 1859), 294-296.

──────. "The Romance of the Negro," *The Galaxy*, XII (October, 1871), 470-478.

──────. "Scraps of Thought," *Southern Literary Messenger*, XVII (March, 1851), 160.

──────. "Stonewall Jackson—An Historical Study," *Putnam's Magazine*, II (December, 1868), 733-740.

──────. "The Story of a California Faro-Table," *Southern Literary Messenger*, XXXII (January, 1861), 37-44.

──────. "The Story of a Hero," *The Galaxy*, VI (November, 1868), 598-605.

──────. "Stray Writings," *Southern Literary Messenger*, XVIII (August, 1852), 468-469.

———. "The Virginia Tourist," *Lippincott's Magazine*, V (May, 1870), 487-497; (June, 1870), 599-609; VI (August, 1870),140-149.

(D) *Personal Periodical*

The Political Pamphlet, New York, September, 1868.

II   *Other Primary Sources*

(A) *Manuscripts*

Archives of the United States
  U.S. Census Manuscripts.
Duke University
  Francis Warrington Dawson Papers.
  Paul Hamilton Hayne Papers.
  William Hahone Papers.
Henry E. Huntington Library
  Robert Alonzo Brock Collection.
Library of Congress
  William Cabell Rives Papers.
University of North Carolina at Chapel Hill
  William Porcher Miles Papers.
University of Virginia
  Daniel-Moncure Papers.
  Hunter-Garnett Papers.
  James Lawson Kemper Papers.
  Edward A. Pollard to Messrs. West and Johnson, May 23, 1863—separate item.
Virginia Historical Society
  George William Bagby Papers.
  Robert Edward Lee Headquarters Papers.
Virginia State Library
  Daniel Harvey Hill Papers.

(B) *Newspapers*

Baltimore *Sun*.
Charleston *Mercury*.
(Columbia, S.C.) *Southern Presbyterian*.
(Leavenworth) *Weekly Kansas Herald*.
Memphis *Avalanche*.
New York *Day-Book*.
New York *Herald*.
New York *Times*.

Bibliography [101]

New York *Tribune.*
Philadelphia *Inquirer.*
Richmond *Dispatch.*
Richmond *Enquirer.*
Richmond *Examiner.*
(Richmond) *Southern Opinion.*
Washington *Union.*

(C) Books

The American Annual Cyclopedia and Register of Important Events, 1872. New York: D. Appleton and Sons, 1872.

Bagby, George W. *The Old Virginia Gentleman and Other Sketches.* Edited with an introduction by Thomas Nelson Page. New York: Charles Scribner's Sons, 1911.

Clemens, Samuel Langhorne ("Mark Twain"). *Life on the Mississippi.* Volume IX of *The Writings of Mark Twain;* New York and London: Harper and Brothers, 1911.

Cooley, Thomas M. *A Treatise on the Constitutional Limitations which Rest upon the Legislative Power of the States of the American Union.* Boston: Little, Brown and Company, 1868.

Dabney, Robert L. *Discussions by Robert L. Dabney, D. D., LL. D., Recently Professor of Moral Philosophy in the University of Texas, and for Many Years Professor of Theology in Union Theological Seminary in Virginia.* Edited by Clement Read Vaughn. Volume IV: *Secular.* Mexico, Mo.: Crescent Publishing House, 1897.

Glasgow, Ellen. *The Deliverance: A Romance of the Virginia Tobacco Fields.* New York: Doubleday, Page and Company, 1904.

Kemble, Edward C. *A History of California Newspapers, 1846-1858.* Edited by Helen Harding Bretnor. Los Gatos, Cal.: Talisman Press, 1962.

Ruffin, Edmund. *Anticipations of the Future, To Serve as Lessons for the Present Time, in the Form of Extracts of Letters from an English Resident of the United States, to the London Times, from 1864 to 1870, with an Appendix, on the Causes and Consequences of the Independence of the South.* Richmond: J. W. Randolph, 1860.

The San Franscisco Directory for 1854. San Francisco: n.p., 1854.

Stowe, Harriet Beecher. *Uncle Tom's Cabin, or Life among the Lowly.* Modern Library edition; New York: Random House, 1938.

Van Evrie, John H. *Negroes and Negro "Slavery": The First an Inferior Race: The Latter Its Normal Condition.* New York: Van Evrie, Horton and Company, 1861.

[102] Bibliography

Walker, William. *The War in Nicaragua.* Mobile, Ala.: S. H. Goetzel, 1860.
Wise, John S. *The End of an Era.* Boston and New York: Houghton Mifflin, 1899.
Withers, Robert E. *The Autobiography of an Octogenarian.* Roanoke, Va.: Stone Printing and Manufacturing Company, 1907.

(D) *Pamphlets*

(Anonymous.) *Papers Showing the Political Course of R. W. Hughes, the Republican Candidate for Governor, before and since the Fall of the Southern Confederacy in 1865; prefixed by a Biographical Sketch.* Richmond: B. W. Gillis, 1873.
Hughes, Robert W. *"Editors of the Past": Lecture of Judge Robert W. Hughes Delivered before the Virginia Press Association at Their Annual Meeting at Charlottesville, Va., on the 22nd of June, 1897.* Richmond: Wm. Ellis Jones, 1897.

(E) *Articles*

Bagby, George W. ("Richard B. Elder"). "Country Life in Virginia Now-a-Days," *Lippincott's Magazine*, IX (March, 1872), 347-351.
Beauregard, Pierre G. T. "Notes on E. A. Pollard's *Lost Cause*, "*The Southern Magazine*, X (January, 1872), 55-64, (February, 1872), 163-71.
Early, Jubal A. "Popular Errors in Regard to the Battles of the War," *The Land We Love*, VI (February, 1869), 265-277.
[Hill, Daniel Harvey]. "The Lost Dispatch," *The Land We Love*, IV (February, 1868), 270-284.
[Van Evrie, John H.] "The Lost Cause," *The Old Guard*, IV (October, 1866), 630-634.

(F) *Public Documents*

Congressional Globe.

(G) *Compilations of Primary Materials*

Cauthen, Charles E., ed., *Family Letters of the Three Wade Hamptons, 1782-1901.* Columbia, S.C.: University of South Carolina Press, 1953.
Chesnut, Mary Boykin. *A Diary from Dixie.* Edited by Ben Ames Williams. Cambridge, Mass.: Houghton Mifflin, 1949.
Dumond, Dwight Lowell, ed. *Southern Editorials on Secession.* New York: Appleton-Century-Crofts, 1931.
Jones, John B. *A Rebel War Clerk's Diary at the Confederate States Capital.* Edited by Howard Swiggett. 2 volumes. New York: Old Hickory Bookshop, 1935.

Myers, Robert Manson, ed. *The Children of Pride: A True Story of Georgia and the Civil War.* New Haven and London: Yale University Press, 1972.
Scott, Robert N., et al., eds. *War of the Rebellion: A Compilation of the Official Records of the Union and Confederate Armies.* 130 volumes. Washington: Government Printing Office, 1880-1901.

II SECONDARY WORKS

(A) Books

Becker, Carl. *The Declaration of Independence: A Study in the History of Political Ideas.* Vintage edition; New York: Vintage Books, 1942.
Boorstin, Daniel J. *The Genius of American Politics.* Chicago: University of Chicago Press, 1953.
Brown, Alexander. *The Cabells and Their Kin: A Memorial Volume of History, Biography, and Genealogy.* Boston and New York: Houghton, Mifflin and Company, 1895.
Buck, Paul H. *The Road to Reunion, 1865-1900.* Boston: Little, Brown and Company, 1937.
Coleman, Charles H. *The Election of 1868: The Democratic Effort to Regain Control.* New York: Columbia University Press, 1933.
Coulter, Ellis Merton. *The Confederate States of America, 1861-1865.* Baton Rouge: Louisiana State University Press, 1950.
DuBois, William E. B. *Black Reconstruction in America: An Essay toward a History of the Part which Black Folk Played in the Attempt to Reconstruct Democracy in America, 1860-1880.* New York: Harcourt Brace, 1935.
Dumond, Dwight Lowell. *The Secession Movement, 1860-1861.* New York: Macmillan, 1931.
Eaton, Clement. *The Waning of the Old South Civilization, 1860-1880.* Athens, Ga.: University of Georgia Press, 1968.
Friedman, Lawrence J. *The White Savage: Racial Fantasies in the Postbellum South.* Englewood Cliffs., N.J.: Prentice-Hall, 1970.
Gaston, Paul M. *The New South Creed: A Study in Southern Mythmaking.* New York: Alfred A. Knopf, 1970.
Glasgow, Ellen. *A Certain Measure: An Interpretation of Prose Fiction.* New York: Harcourt, Brace and Company, 1938.
Hartz, Louis. *The Liberal Tradition in America.* New York: Harcourt Brace and World, 1955.
King, Alvy L. *Louis T. Wigfall: Southern Fire-Eater.* Baton Rouge: Louisiana State University Press, 1970.
Maddex, Jack P., Jr. *The Virginia Conservatives, 1867-1879: A*

Study in Reconstruction Politics. Chapel Hill: University of North Carolina Press, 1970.

Marx, Karl, and Frederick Engels. *Selected Works.* 2 volumes. Moscow: Foreign Languages Publishing House, 1962.

Nichols, Roy F. *The Disruption of American Democracy.* New York: Macmillan, 1948.

Odum, Howard W. *Southern Regions of the United States.* Chapel Hill: University of North Carolina Press, 1936.

Phillips, Ulrich B. *The Course of the South to Secession.* Edited by E. Merton Coulter. New York and London: D. Appleton-Century Company, 1939.

Pressly, Thomas J. *Americans Interpret Their Civil War.* Princeton: Princeton University Press, 1954.

Rawley, James A. *Race and Politics: "Bleeding Kansas" and the Coming of the Civil War.* Philadelphia and New York: J. B. Lippincott Company, 1970.

Takaki, Ronald T. *A Pro-Slavery Crusade: The Agitation to Reopen the African Slave Trade.* New York: Free Press, 1971.

Thompson, William Y. *Robert Toombs of Georgia.* Baton Rouge: Louisiana State University Press, 1966.

Wilson, Edmund. *Patriotic Gore: Studies in the Literature of the American Civil War.* New York: Oxford University Press, 1962.

Wood, Forrest G. *Black Scare: The Racist Response to Emancipation and Reconstruction.* Berkeley and Los Angeles: University of California Press, 1968.

Woodward, C. Vann. *The Origins of the New South, 1877-1913.* Baton Rouge: Louisiana State University Press, 1951.

Woodward, C. Vann. *The Strange Career of Jim Crow.* New York: Oxford University Press, 1955.

(B) Articles

Davis, C. C. "Elegant Old Rebel," *Virginia Cavalcade,* VIII (summer, 1958), 42-47.

Genovese, Eugené D. "Race and Class in Southern History: An Appraisal of the Work of Ulrich Bonnell Phillips," *Agricultural History,* XLI (October, 1967), 345-358.

Govan, Thomas P. "Was the Old South Different?", *Journal of Southern History,* XXI (November, 1955), 447-455.

Hamilton, James Gregoire de Roulhac. "Edward Alfred Pollard," in Allen Johnson and Dumas Malone, eds., *Dictionary of American Biography* (22 volumes; New York: Charles Scribner's Sons, 1928-1937), XV, 47-48.

Luraghi, Raimondo. "The Civil War and the Modernization of American Society: Social Structure and Industrial Revolution in

the Old South before and during the Civil War," *Civil War History,* *XVIII* (September, 1972), 230-250.
Phillips, Ulrich B. "The Central Theme of Southern History," *American Historical Review,* XXXIV (October, 1928), 30-43.
Van Auken, Sheldon. "The Southern Historical Novel in the Early Twentieth Century," *Journal of Southern History,* XIV (May, 1948), 157-191.
Wilson, James Southall. "Edward Alfred Pollard," in Edwin A. Alderman, Joel Chandler Harris, and Charles Kent, eds., *Library of Southern Literature, Compiled under the Supervision of Southern Men of Letters* (16 volumes; New Orleans, Atlanta, and Dallas: Martin and Hoyt, 1907), IX, 4147-4150.

(C) *Unpublished Theses*

Houston, Michael. "Edward A. Pollard and the Richmond *Examiner;* A Study of Journalistic Opposition in Wartime," M. A. thesis, American University, 1963.
Wiener, Jonathan. "Plantations, Politics, and Industry: Alabama, 1850-1890." Ph.D. dissertation, Harvard University, 1972.

INDEX

A
Aaron, Black (character), 28
Africa, 14, 29, 74
Albemarle County (Va.), 4
Alta Vista plantation, 4
American Revolution, 53, 56
"Anti-Slavery Men of the South, The," 77-78, 83
Appleton's Annual Cyclopedia, 78
Asia, 4, 35
Atlanta, 17

B
Bagby, George W., 74
Baltimore, 4, 6
Baltimore *Sun*, 4
Baptist church, 82
Bell, Henry H., 69
Birmingham, 17
Black Codes, 75
Black Diamonds, 4, 7, 26, 77, 84
Blake, Mrs. (character), 82, 84
Blease, Cole, 16
Boston, 5
Britain, 5, 27
Brooklyn, 5
Brown, John, 14
Buchanan, James, 67

C
Calhoun, John C., 16, 41; Pollard on, 40, 45, 53, 76, 83
California, 4, 24-25, 44, 73
Caribbean, 4, 25-26, 29
"Central Theme of Southern History, The" (Phillips), 8-9, 80-81
Chase, Salmon P., 45
Clarkson, David M., 28
Confederate States of America, 3, 7, 15, 30-33, 43; retrospective interpretations, 20-22; *see also* Pollard, Edward A., opinions
Congress (C.S.), 47, 65
Congress (U.S.), 34, 37, 53-54, 57
Conservative Unionism, 14-15, 21, 22, 68; *see also* Democratic Party, and Pollard, Edward A., opinions
"Constitutional liberty" concept, 44-45, 50, 53-55, 64, 67-68, 84
Cooley, Thomas M., 55
"Copperheads," 41, 55, 60
Crittenden, John J., 67

D
Daniel, John Moncure, 4-5
Davis, Jefferson, 3, 6, 16, 31; Pollard on, 34-37, 46-47, 61, 64-68, 71, 76-77
Declaration of Independence, 70
Deliverance, The (Glasgow), 82
Democratic National Convention (1868), 46, 56
Democratic Party, 6, 22, 44, 82; *see also* Pollard, Edward A., opinions
Dorr Rebellion, 12
Douglas, Stephen A., 67
DuBois, William E. Burghardt, 18

E
Echoes from the South, 6, 35, 37
Emancipation Proclamation, 32
Episcopal church, 4
Eva (character), 13

F
Fisher, Sidney G., 8
Fitzhugh, George, 12
Foote, Henry S., 71-72
Fort Sumter, 20, 30, 67
Fortress Monroe, 5
Fourteenth Amendment, 52

G
Glasgow, Ellen, 82
"Good Old Rebel, The" (Randolph), 36
Grant, James, 6, 63
Grant, Ulysses S., 63, 71, 79
Greeley, Horace, 71

Index

H
Hammond, James H., 59
Hampden-Sidney College, 4
Hayne, Paul Hamilton, 74
Henry, Patrick, 76
Hill, Daniel Harvey, 6
Hughes, Robert W., 61

J
Jackson, Thomas J. ("Stonewall"), 65
Jefferson, Thomas, 44-45, 53, 76
Jefferson Davis, Life of, see *Life of Jefferson Davis*
Jesus, 57
Johnson, Andrew, 34, 44-45, 47-48, 55, 57, 67, 70
Judiciary Committee (House of Representatives), 4

K
Kansas, 25
Ku Klux Klan, 75

L
Lee, Robert E., 3, 5, 22; Pollard on, 65, 67
Lee and His Lieutenants, 6, 35
Letcher, John, 30
Letters of the Southern Spy, 4
Liberal Republican Party, 71, 78
Life of Jefferson Davis, 6, 64-69
Lincoln, Abraham, 4, 11, 13-14, 30, 32, 47, 66-67
"Living Politicians of To-Day, The," 45
Lost Cause, The, 5-7, 35, 37-38, 45
"Lost Cause Regained" idea, 8-9, 23, 43, 47, 50-58, 60-62, 64, 67-69, 76-78, 80, 83-84
Lost Cause Regained, The, 6, 8-9, 23, 43, 45-64, 69, 77-78, 80-81, 83
Louisiana Lottery Company, 22
Lynchburg, (Va.), 6-7
Lynchburg *Republican*, 7

M
Marx, Karl, 83
Memphis *Avalanche*, 5
Methodist church, 6
Milton, John, 57
Montgomery Convention, 66-67
Montgomery *Post*, 14-15

N
Nelson County (Va.), 4
"New South" slogan, 17-19, 72
"New Virginia" slogan, 72
New York, 6, 12, 25, 46, 56, 63
New York *Times*, 3
New York *Tribune*, 71
New York *World*, 71
Nicaragua, 25
Northern society, 11-12; see also Pollard, Edward A., opinions

O
Oakridge plantation, 4, 27, 78-79
Observations in the North, 5
Orr, James L., 35

P
Paradise Regained (Milton), 57
Pendleton, George H., 45
Phillips, Ulrich B., 8-9, 80-81
Political Pamphlet, The, 62
Pollard family, 4
Pollard, Edward A., birth, 4, 24; education, 4; California career, 4, 24-25; travels, 4-5, 7, 25; association with William Walker, 25; marriages, 4-6, 43; break with Union, 4, 30; journalistic work, 4-6, 30, 62; wartime captivity, 5, 32; postwar imprisonment, 5, 33; 1868 campaign efforts, 62-63; custom-house position, 6, 63; effort to convict brother's murderer, 6, 63; Lynchburg residence, 6-7; death, 7, 78; contemporary reputation, 5-7; subsequent reputation, 3, 7-9; "falsification of memory," 83-84;
OPINIONS: on slavery, 24-29, 32, 38-39, 50-52, 61, 64, 71, 76-78; on African slave trade, 29; on Southern civilization, 26-27, 35, 38-39, 47-48, 52; on Caribbean expansion, 25-26, 29; on Southern nationalism, 29-32, 35-38, 41-43, 45, 47-48; on secession and War's origin, 30-31, 38, 40, 45, 48, 60-61, 66-67, 76; on Confederacy, 30-33, 36, 40, 46-47, 50-54, 57-58, 60-61, 64-69, 76-77; on Northern society, 24-25, 27, 30, 39, 72-73; on public

Index [109]

schools, 39, 73; on Union, 29-31, 39-40, 44, 45, 48-49, 48-60, 70; on patriotic symbols, 40, 59, 69; on U.S. Constitution, 40, 48-50, 53-54, 62-63, 70-71; on U.S. government, 32, 40, 57, 59-60; on loyalty oaths, 33, 63, 84; on Reconstruction policy, 37, 44, 49-50, 52, 56-57, 70, 75; on Republican Party, 30-31, 34, 45-50, 55, 62, 71-72; on Democratic party, 25, 29, 31, 40-41, 46, 54-56, 58-59, 62-63, 70-71; on Liberal Republican party, 71; on conservative Unionists, 34-35, 40-41, 44-45, 47-49, 54-58; on race, 27-28, 38, 48-52, 55, 57, 64, 68, 74-76, 78; on civil rights, 52, 75; on "constitutional liberty," 49-50, 53-55, 67-68; on state rights, 40-41, 48, 53, 55, 70-71; on presidency, 53-54; on Southern political violence, 37, 56-57, 75-76; on postwar Southern needs, 35-37, 57-58, 71-73; on social norms, 73; on Virginia social geography, 73-74; on literary style, 74; on individuals, *see* their names
Pollard, H. Rives, 4-6, 24-25, 33, 35, 44, 46, 63, 78
Pollard, John, 24
Pollard, Marie A. N. G. D., 5-6
Pollard, Richard, 6-7
Pomeroy, Marcus M. ("Brick"), 70

R
Randolph, Innes, 36
Reconstruction program, 21; *see also* Pollard, Edward A., opinions
Regionalism, concepts of, 9-10, 15
"Rent wars," 12
Republican National Convention (1868), 46
Republican Party, 15, 21. 25-26; *see also* Pollard, Edward A., opinions
Richmond, 4-6, 30, 35, 63, 82
Richmond *Examiner*, 3-5, 7, 30, 61
Rienzi, Cola di, 84
Rives family, 4
Rives, Alexander, 79
Ruffin, Edmund, 20

S
Samford, William F., 37
Scott, Sir Walter, 74
Secession, 6, 14-15, 30; *see also* Pollard, Edward A., opinions
Seward, William H., 45
Seymour, Horatio, 62
Slavery, 11, 16, 18, 80-81; Southern commitment to, as good, 12-15; *see also* Pollard, Edward A., opinions
South, concept, 9-10; antebellum society and culture, 10-15, 81-82; postbellum society and culture, 15-20, 82-84; *see also* Pollard, Edward A., opinions
South Carolina, 11
Southern Commercial Convention (1856), 26
Southern History of the War, 5, 33-34
Southern nationalism, 8-9, 12, 16-17, 68, 80-81; *see also* Pollard, Edward A., opinions
Southern Opinion, 6, 35, 41, 44
State rights, 17; *see also* Pollard, Edward A., opinions
Stephens, Alexander H., 67
Stowe, Harriet Beecher, 13
Suez Canal, 72

T
Tilden, Samuel J., 55
Toombs, Robert, 47, 67, 71
Transcendentalism, 12
Treatise on Constitutional Limitations (Cooley), 55

V
Van Evrie, John H., 51-52, 55, 60
Vardaman, James K., 16
Virginia, 4, 30, 44, 56, 72-73
Virginia, University of, 4
Virginia Tourist, The, 6, 72
Voorhees, Daniel W., 71

W
War of 1861-65, 3, 10, 17-18, 30-33, 81, 82, 84; retrospective interpretations, 21-22; *see also* Pollard, Edward A., opinions
Washington (D.C.), 4, 30

Weekly Kansas Herald, 25
"White supremacy" concept, 8-9, 13, 17, 27-28, 48, 50-52, 54-55, 68, 76, 80, 84
Wiener, Jonathan, 18
Wigfall, Louis T., 67
William and Mary, College of, 4
Wilson, Henry, 55
Wise, Henry A., 6, 35, 71
Woodward, C. Vann, 22, 81

Y

Yancey, William L., 67

www.ingramcontent.com/pod-product-compliance
Lightning Source LLC
Chambersburg PA
CBHW030117010526
44116CB00005B/295